Heinemann is an imprint of Pearson Education Limited, a company
incorporated in England and Wales, having its registered office at Edinburgh
Gate, Harlow, Essex, CM20 2JE. Registered company number: 872828

Heinemann is a registered trademark of Pearson Education Limited

The publishers and Series Editor are indebted to James Reeves for his work as
Founding Editor of the original Poetry Bookshelf series.

10 09 08
9 8 7

A catalogue record for this book is available from the British Library on
request.

ISBN: 978 0 435150 81 5

Cover design by The Point

Text design by Roger Davies

Typeset by Books Unlimited (Nottm)

Printed in China by CTPS/07

CONTENTS

Introduction   vii

John Donne

Elegy: To his Mistress Going to Bed	1
Elegy: On his Mistress	3
The Flea	7
The Good Morrow	9
Song (Go, and catch . . .)	11
The Undertaking	13
The Sun Rising	15
The Canonization	17
Song (Sweetest love . . .)	19
Air and Angels	21
The Anniversary	23
Twickenham Garden	25
A Valediction: of Weeping	27
A Nocturnal upon St Lucy's Day	29
A Valediction: forbidding Mourning	33
The Funeral	35
The Relic	37
The Prohibition	39
The Expiration	41
Holy Sonnets : This is my play's . . .	41
At the round earth's . . .	43
Death be not proud . . .	43
What if this present . . .	45
Batter my heart . . .	45
I am a little world . . .	47
Since she whom I loved . . .	47
Oh, to vex me . . .	49

Good Friday 1613. Riding Westward   49
A Hymn to God the Father   53

George Herbert

The Church-Floor   57
The Windows   57
Christmas   59
Good Friday   61
Easter   63
Jordan (I)   65
Jordan (II)   67
Aaron   67
Prayer (I)   69
The Pearl   71
Man   73
Life   77
Mortification   79
The Pulley   81
Death   83
Redemption   85
Affliction (I)   85
Denial   89
The Collar   91
Love (III)   95

Thomas Carew

An Elegy upon the Death of the Dean of Paul's, Dr John Donne   99
Mediocrity in Love Rejected   105
To My Inconstant Mistress   105
Persuasions to enjoy   107
Boldness in Love   107
A Song   109

Richard Crashaw

A Hymn of the Navity, sung as by the Shepherds 113
Hymn to Saint Teresa 121

Andrew Marvell

On a Drop of Dew 135
Bermudas 137
The Nymph complaining for the death of her Fawn 139
The Definition of Love 147
To his Coy Mistress 149
The Fair Singer 151
The Picture of little T.C. in a Prospect of Flowers 153
The Garden 155
An Horatian Ode upon Cromwell's Return from Ireland 161

Henry Vaughan

Regeneration 171
The Retreat 175
The Morning-watch 177
The Dawning 179
The World 183
Man 185
Cock-crowing 187
The Night 191
The Waterfall 195

Chronological Table 199
Critical Approaches 201
Exploration and Discussion 211
Essay Topics 236
Writing an Essay About Poetry 237

A Note from a Chief Examiner   239

Select Bibliography   243

Index of First Lines   245

INTRODUCTION

The lives of the poets whose work appears in this volume span over one hundred years, from the birth of John Donne in 1572 to the death of Henry Vaughan in 1695. These poets experienced, and contributed to, the culture and events which constitute the spirit of the turbulent era in which they lived. Each responded to it in his own way, in life and in art, providing contemporary (and succeeding) readers with writings which can provoke, entertain, challenge, frustrate and delight – sometimes all at the same time. Undoubtedly, these poets share many similarities of subject-matter and technique, but each of them is unique.

These poets have been labelled 'metaphysical', a term which was attached to many seventeenth-century poets, and their work, long after their deaths. They did not use it of themselves, nor was it current during their lifetimes. As none of them consciously set out to write a metaphysical poem, it is perhaps best to respond to each poet, and to each poem, without attempting to assess how they fit a definition imposed by later generations. The designation has been retained in the title of this selection because of its familiarity: it is still widely recognized as defining, however loosely, a number of writers whose work exhibits certain shared literary and philosophical approaches.

This edition contains a selection of the work of six poets: Donne, Herbert, Carew, Crashaw, Marvell and Vaughan. The poems have been chosen to provide examples of a range of writing, including some of these poets' best-known work, together with poems which are, perhaps, less familiar. Glossary notes are printed opposite the text, together with points for consideration, to stimulate initial thinking about some aspects of each poem. Suggestions for exploration and discussion, and the **Critical Approaches** section at the end of this edition, will, it is hoped, provide readers and students with information and ideas to encourage close reading, and help them to formulate informed personal responses.

John Donne (1572 – 1631)

John Donne was born in London, the third child of a Catholic family. His father, a successful ironmonger, died when Donne was four. His mother's second husband was a notable physician, also Catholic. The position of Catholics in England during the reign of Elizabeth I was both complex and dangerous. It was possible to escape the notice of the authorities, to enjoy a successful career and reasonable security, but with difficulty. Huge fines were levied on Catholics who refused to attend Anglican services. It was high treason for a Catholic priest to be within the Queen's dominions, and a felony to harbour a priest. Thus, a Catholic could not, legally, make confession or hear Mass. The financial penalties which Catholic suspects suffered were negligible compared with the horrors of torture and execution suffered by condemned felons, and all Catholics were in constant danger of betrayal.

John Donne grew from child to man under the shadow of this threat, and with the images of martyrdom always before him. His mother was a collateral descendant of Sir Thomas More, the Lord Chancellor whom Henry VIII had executed for his opposition to the king's defiance of the Roman Catholic church. Two of Donne's uncles were Jesuits, and one of them was sentenced to death (later commuted to banishment) for high treason. Donne's elder brother, Henry, was imprisoned in 1593 for harbouring a priest, and died of the plague in Newgate.

Donne's education was with private Catholic tutors, next briefly at Cambridge, then as a law student in London. He appears to have been popular with his young contemporaries, being chosen Master of the Revels at Lincoln's Inn. The image of 'Jack' Donne, the lad-about-town, 'a great visitor of ladies, a great frequenter of plays, a great writer of conceited verses' (as an acquaintance described him) comes from this time. It is the picture of Donne that has sometimes dominated and obscured more important aspects of his character, life and writing, though it has undoubted immediate appeal, particularly when seen in combination with the romantic visual image presented by the portrait painted of him in his youth (known as the Lothian portrait) and the 'masculine persuasive force' of the love lyrics.

In 1596–7 Donne sailed as a volunteer with the Earl of Essex in expeditions against the Spanish, and late in 1597 he returned to England and became secretary to Sir Thomas Egerton, Lord Keeper of the Seal. He then met his patron's niece, Ann More. In 1601 they were secretly married, and thus Donne effectively ruined all chance of a career in public or private service for many years to come. His abject letter pleading for forgiveness to Ann's father, Sir George More, states: '. . . if you incense my Lord [Egerton], you destroy her and me . . .', and this proved true.

Dismissed from his post, briefly imprisoned in the Fleet, Donne spent the next thirteen years without regular employment, and was frequently suicidal. He had a few influential friends and some limited short-term employment, but his lack of proper occupation often drove him to despair. He lived in a small, damp house at Mitcham, south of London, with an increasing family; Ann died in 1617, bearing their twelfth child. Yet one of the many paradoxes of Donne's life as a man and as a poet is that it seems that the majority of the *Songs and Sonnets* come from this unhappy period. There is no evidence which points to earlier composition. It also appears that his love for Ann was unshaken.

In 1615 Donne was ordained a priest. He had, by then, rejected Catholicism. Was this from expediency or conviction? It is tempting to suggest that Donne's keen and rational mind rejected the superstitions and miracles which demanded blind faith. In *Satire III*, written around 1594–5 (well before his hope of a successful secular career had faded), he concludes: 'So perish souls, which more choose men's unjust/Power from God claimed, than God himself to trust.' Donne was appointed Dean of St Paul's in 1621, and gained the reputation of an outstanding preacher. His sermons, and the late religious poems, show that though he may have set aside the vibrant wit and sexual arrogance of his youth, the generative force of his intelligence and imagination was undimmed.

Donne's life was full of change and instability. Truth confronted unfaithfulness; where did either reside? Who, or what, could be trusted? Men and women, religion and emotion, profane and sacred love, life itself – all are mutable, and Donne's intense awareness of this, and his analysis of himself and his place in this shifting world, give his poetry its unique voice and vitality.

Elegy: To his Mistress Going to Bed

Donne's poems were not published in his lifetime, although several of his sermons were. After his death, his son had an edition of the poems printed in 1633, and a second, enlarged, edition in 1635.

Donne's love elegies are early writings, and can be dated between about 1593 and his marriage in 1601. Many of them celebrate sexual adventures and present a picture of a libertine, a risk-taking young man, exploring and exploiting his opportunities and recording them (whether they be fact or fiction) with equal wit and energy.

> *What impression does the speaker in this poem give of himself, and of the woman he is addressing?*

- 5   *heaven's zone* – the Milky Way.
- 7   *spangled breastplate* – stomacher, set with jewels. The martial implications of the word Donne chooses link with the military language, used to refer to his erect penis, in lines 3-4.
- 9   *harmonious chime* – the chiming of a clock or, more likely, the sounds made by her jewelled clothing as she undresses.
- 11 *busk* – corset
- 12 *still can be, and still can stand* – the play on words refers to the rigidity of the corset, and of his erection.
- 14 *meads* – meadows.
- 15–16 *wiry coronet ... hairy diadem* – fashionable caps or head-ornaments were often constructed on a wire framework. Donne contrasts the artificial (clothed) with the natural (naked), a theme which is pursued throughout the poem.
- 21 *Mahomet's paradise* – a feature of the Muslim paradise was thought to be beautiful maidens, or houris.
- 22 *Ill spirits walk in white* – it was thought difficult to distinguish between bad and good spirits, as the former could disguise themselves.
- 24 *our flesh upright* – an overt reference to the male erection.
- 25 *Licence* – give licence to …, but, looking forward to the following lines, there is also an implication of giving a franchise to discover and exploit, as many merchant venturers and explorers were doing at that time.
- 27 *my America, my new found land* – exploration and exploitation of America by Europeans, especially the Spanish, Portuguese, Dutch and English, was in full swing.

Elegy: To his Mistress Going to Bed

Come, Madam, come, all rest my powers defy,
Until I labour, I in labour lie.
The foe oft-times, having the foe in sight,
Is tired with standing, though they never fight.
5 Off with that girdle, like heaven's zone glistering,
But a far fairer world encompassing.
Unpin that spangled breastplate, which you wear
That th'eyes of busy fools may be stopped there:
Unlace yourself, for that harmonious chime
10 Tells me from you that now 'tis your bed-time.
Off with that happy busk, which I envy,
That still can be, and still can stand so nigh.
Your gown's going off such beauteous state reveals,
As when from flowery meads th'hills shadow steals.
15 Off with your wiry coronet and show
The hairy diadem which on you doth grow.
Off with those shoes: and then safely tread
In this love's hallowed temple, this soft bed.
In such white robes heaven's angels used to be
20 Received by men; thou angel bring'st with thee
A heaven like Mahomet's paradise; and though
Ill spirits walk in white, we easily know
By this these angels from an evil sprite,
They set our hairs, but these our flesh upright.
25   Licence my roving hands, and let them go
Behind, before, above, between, below.
O my America, my new found land,
My kingdom, safeliest when with one man manned,
My mine of precious stones, my empery,
30 How blessed am I in this discovering thee.
To enter in these bonds is to be free,
Then where my hand is set my seal shall be.
  Full nakedness, all joys are due to thee.
As souls unbodied, bodies unclothed must be,

36 *Atlanta's balls* – in Greek myth, Atlanta was a swift-footed maiden who refused to marry anyone who could not defeat her in a race. Aphrodite, the goddess of love, gave the golden apples of the Hesperides to Hippomenes, who dropped them at strategic points during the race, knowing that Atlanta would stop to pick them up. Donne has here subverted the legend so that it is men, rather than women, who are distracted by baubles.

38 *covet theirs, not them* – a foolish man is distracted by the jewels which women wear, ignoring the beauty of their unadorned bodies.

41–42 *mystic books … imputed grace* – women are books which contain secrets which they will reveal only to those to whom they grant grace. The term 'imputed grace' is drawn from Calvinist theology, the grace through which the merits of Christ are imputed to the righteous.

46 *no penance, much less innocence* – white clothing was worn by public penitents. The first printed text of this poem read 'no penance due to innocence', which gives a rather different impression of the woman's previous sexual experience.

48 *than a man* – the word-play implies that he is naked and that she is covered by him.

Elegy: On His Mistress

The probable composition date of this poem (1599–1601) invites speculation. Donne had met his future wife, Ann, in 1597, but their relationship was secret until their marriage in December 1601. The mistress-disguised-as-page theme is a common one: Shakespeare used it in plays such as *Twelfth Night*, and fictional material, presented dramatically, can be very convincing.

Does this read like a poem of genuine persuasion?

1 *fatal* – ordained by Fate.

3 *remorse* – compassion.

8 *want and divorcement* – lacking and separation (from each other).

14 *feigned page* – disguised as his page.

35 To taste whole joys. Gems which you women use
    Are as Atlanta's balls, cast in men's views,
    That when a fool's eye lighteth on a gem
    His earthly soul may covet theirs, not them.
    Like pictures, or like books' gay coverings made
40 For laymen, are all women thus arrayed;
    Themselves are mystic books, which only we
    Whom their imputed grace will dignify
    Must see revealed. Then since I may know,
    As liberally as to a midwife show
45 Thyself; cast all, yea this white linen hence,
    Here is no penance, much less innocence.
        To teach thee, I am naked first: why then
    What needst thou have more covering than a man?

Elegy: On his Mistress

    By our first strange and fatal interview,
    By all desires which thereof did ensue,
    By our long starving hopes, by that remorse
    Which my words' masculine persuasive force
5   Begot in thee, and by the memory
    Of hurts which spies and rivals threatened me,
    I calmly beg; but by thy parents' wrath,
    By all pains which want and divorcement hath,
    I conjure thee; and all those oaths which I
10 And thou have sworn, to seal joint constancy,
    Here I unswear, and overswear them thus:
    Thou shalt not love by means so dangerous.
    Temper, oh fair love, love's impetuous rage,
    Be my true mistress still, not my feigned page.
15 I'll go, and, by thy kind leave, leave behind
    Thee, only worthy to nurse in my mind
    Thirst to come back; oh, if thou die before,
    From other lands my soul towards thee shall soar,
    Thy (else almighty) beauty cannot move

21–3   *Boreas ... Orithea* – in the Greek myth, Boreas, the north wind, carried Orithea away, and in some versions she marries him and bears his children. Plato, in *Phaedrus*, has her blown over a cliff and killed.

25   *flattery* – not the modern meaning of insincere praise; the implication is more of hope, something which soothes fears.

27   *Dissemble ... not a boy* – disguise nothing, do not pretend to be a boy.

28–9   *be not strange/To thy self only* – the implication is that she will only deceive herself.

33–4   *Men of France ... Spitals of diseases* – spitals are hospitals; the implication is that the French are full of diseases, probably venereal. The descriptions of the French, the Italians and, later, the Dutch are xenophobic caricatures of these nationalities.

37   *know thee, and know thee* – a play on words: recognize her as a woman and rape her.

38   *indifferent* – bisexual.

41   *Lot's fair guests* – Genesis 19. Lot was visited by two angels at his house in Sodom, where they were besieged by the men of the city who wished to rape the strangers.

42   *spongy hydroptic Dutch* – refers to the waterlogged state of Holland.

44   *England is only a worthy gallery* – i.e. only England is (etc.). A gallery was a long room, frequently a waiting-room adjoining the state rooms, where a king would receive courtiers or petitioners.

46   *our great King* – possibly a personification of love. In *The Ecstasy* Donne refers to love as 'a great prince'.

55   *Augur* – predict.

20 Rage from the seas, nor thy love teach them love,
Nor tame wild Boreas' harshness; thou hast read
How roughly he in pieces shivered
Fair Orithea, whom he swore he loved.
Fall ill or good, 'tis madness to have proved

25 Dangers unurged; feed on this flattery,
That absent lovers one in th'other be.
Dissemble nothing, not a boy, nor change
Thy body's habit, nor mind's; be not strange
To thy self only; all will spy in thy face

30 A blushing womanly discovering grace.
Richly clothed apes are called apes, and as soon
Eclipsed as bright, we call the moon, the moon.
Men of France, changeable chameleons,
Spitals of diseases, shops of fashions,

35 Love's fuellers, and the rightest company
Of players which upon the world's stage be,
Will quickly know thee, and know thee; and alas
Th'indifferent Italian, as we pass
His warm land, well content to think thee page,

40 Will haunt thee, with such lust and hideous rage
As Lot's fair guests were vexed: but none of these
Nor spongy hydroptic Dutch, shall thee displease,
If thou stay here. Oh stay here, for, for thee
England is only a worthy gallery,

45 To walk in expectation, till from thence
Our great King call thee into his presence.
When I am gone, dream me some happiness,
Nor let thy looks our long-hid love confess,
Nor praise, nor dispraise me, nor bless nor curse

50 Openly love's force; nor in bed fright thy nurse
With midnight's startings, crying out, 'Oh, oh,
Nurse, oh my love is slain; I saw him go
O'er the white Alps, alone; I saw him, I,
Assailed, fight, taken, stabbed, bleed, fall, and die.'

55 Augur me better chance, except dread Jove
Think it enough for me, to have had thy love.

Songs and Sonnets

The dating of these poems is conjectural, but some deductions can be made from the content and context of many of the poems, and these suggest a date post-1602, after Donne's marriage. References to the king appear in *The Sun Rising, The Canonization* and *The Anniversary*. James I came to the throne in 1603. Lady Bedford, who is linked with *Twickenham Garden* and *A Nocturnal upon St Lucy's Day*, lived in Twickenham from 1607.

The Flea

The flea was a frequent subject in sixteenth- and seventeenth-century European poetry.

How does the form of this poem reflect its content?

  6   *maidenhead* – virginity.

18   *sacrilege, three sins* – two murders (the flea and the poet) and suicide: the repetition of 'three' has resonances of the Trinity, so a hint of blasphemy can be read also.

27   waste – be lost.

The Flea

Mark but this flea, and mark in this,
How little that which thou deny'st me is;
Me it sucked first, and now sucks thee,
And in this flea, our two bloods mingled be;
5 Thou know'st that this cannot be said
A sin, or shame, or loss of maidenhead,
    Yet this enjoys before it woo,
    And pampered swells with one blood made of two,
    And this, alas, is more than we would do.

10 Oh stay, three lives in one flea spare,
Where we almost, nay more than married are.
This flea is you, and I, and this
Our marriage bed, and marriage temple is;
Though parents grudge, and you, we'are met,
15 And cloistered in these living walls of jet.
    Though use make you apt to kill me,
    Let not to this, self murder added be,
    And sacrilege, three sins in killing three.

Cruel and sudden, hast thou since
20 Purpled thy nail, in blood of innocence?
In what could this flea guilty be,
Except in that drop which it sucked from thee?
Yet thou triumph'st, and say'st that thou
Find'st not thyself, nor me the weaker now;
25   'Tis true, then learn how false fears be;
    Just so much honour, when thou yield'st to me,
    Will waste, as this flea's death took life from thee.

The Good Morrow

Note how the tone of the opening is determined by the syntax, a series of questions followed by an affirmative clause. What mood is then created in the succeeding lines and stanzas?

3   *country* – as so often with the use of this word in sixteenth- and seventeenth-century writing, an indecent pun is intended.

4   *seven sleepers* – a Christian legend tells of seven young men of Ephesus, who were walled up alive during religious persecution, and slept for 187 years.

5   *fancies* – delusions.

17   *hemispheres* – the two halves of the earth.

19   *whatever dies, was not mixed equally* – only those things which are compounded of elements mixed in perfect proportions are immortal. Contemporary medical theory ascribed disease to an imbalance of the humours (which had their source in the elements) within the body.

The Good Morrow

I wonder by my troth, what thou, and I
    Did, till we loved? were we not weaned till then,
But sucked on country pleasures, childishly?
    Or snorted we in the seven sleepers' den?
5 'Twas so; but this, all pleasures fancies be.
    If ever any beauty I did see,
Which I desired, and got, 'twas but a dream of thee.

And now good morrow to our waking souls,
    Which watch not one another out of fear;
10 For love, all love of other sights controls,
    And makes one little room, an everywhere.
Let sea-discoverers to new worlds have gone,
Let maps to others, worlds on worlds have shown,
Let us possess one world, each hath one, and is one.

15 My face in thine eye, thine in mine appears,
    And true plain hearts do in the faces rest,
Where can we find two better hemispheres
    Without sharp north, without declining west?
Whatever dies, was not mixed equally;
20 If our two loves be one, or, thou and I
Love so alike, that none do slacken, none can die.

Song (Go, and catch ...)

As in *The Flea*, Donne uses nine-line stanzas, but in a different form.

2 *mandrake* – the mandrake was believed to have mystic and magical properties. Its forked shape was popularly believed to resemble a man's legs and genitals, and it was thought that it grew from the spilt sperm of a hanged man. It was also believed to shriek when pulled from the ground. It was used both as an aphrodisiac and an abortifacient. It is poisonous. With all its attributed properties, its frequent literary references (also as mandragora) are not surprising.

Does this read as a light-hearted, or a serious, poem?

Song

Go, and catch a falling star,
   Get with child a mandrake root,
Tell me, where all past years are,
   Or who cleft the Devil's foot,
5 Teach me to hear mermaids singing,
   Or to keep off envy's stinging,
         And find
         What wind
Serves to advance an honest mind.

10 If thou be'est born to strange sights,
   Things invisible to see,
Ride ten thousand days and nights,
   Till age snow white hairs on thee.
Thou, when thou return'st, wilt tell me
15 All strange wonders that befell thee,
         And swear
         Nowhere
Lives a woman true, and fair.

If thou find'st one, let me know,
20   Such a pilgrimage were sweet;
Yet do not, I would not go,
   Though at next door we might meet,
Though she were true, when you met her,
And last, till you write your letter,
25   Yet she
         Will be
False, ere I come, to two, or three.

The Undertaking

The analogy between the simple quatrains and circular form of this poem and what the poet is saying is straightforward and self-evident: the recognition that beauty does not depend on outward form, that inner virtue should be most prized, and that the discovery of this should not be boasted of.

2   *worthies* – legendary warriors.

6   *specular stone* – this was thought to be a transparent stone used in ancient times for the building of temples.

17–20   *If, as I have … He and She* – Donne suggests in this stanza that virtue is a quality which can be found in woman, and that this revelation enables one to transcend gender or sexuality.

The Undertaking

I have done one braver thing
    Than all the Worthies did,
And yet a braver thence doth spring,
    Which is, to keep that hid.

5 It were but madness now t'impart
    The skill of specular stone,
When he which can have learned the art
    To cut it, can find none.

So, if I now should utter this,
10   Others (because no more
Such stuff to work upon, there is,)
    Would love but as before.

But he who loveliness within
    Hath found, all outward loathes,
15 For he who colour loves, and skin,
    Loves but their oldest clothes.

If, as I have, you also do
    Virtue attired in woman see,
And dare love that, and say so too,
20   And forget the He and She;

And if this love, though placed so,
    From profane men you hide,
Which will no faith on this bestow,
    Or, if they do, deride:

25 Then you have done a braver thing
    Than all the Worthies did,
And a braver thence will spring,
    Which is, to keep that hid.

The Sun Rising

The arrogant, amused belittling of the sun is a device to accentuate and aggrandize the poet and the woman.

7   *court-huntsmen, that the King will ride* – James I was passionate about hunting. The reference suggests a date after 1603.

9   *all alike ... clime* – unchanging, knows no climate, or region.

17 *Indias of spice and mine* – the East and West Indies; the West Indies were exploited for gold, the East for spices.

24 *mimic* – imitation.
    alchemy – (here) false gold.

30 *This bed thy centre is, these walls thy sphere* – Donne draws on a geocentric (Ptolemaic) model of the universe, though by the date of this poem the heliocentric (Copernican) model was generally accepted. The geocentric model provided far more useful images for poets.

What is the importance of concepts of time and space in this poem?

The Sun Rising

       Busy old fool, unruly sun,
        Why dost thou thus,
Through windows, and through curtains call on us?
Must to thy motions lovers' seasons run?
5   Saucy pedantic wretch, go chide
       Late schoolboys, and sour prentices,
Go tell court-huntsmen, that the King will ride,
Call country ants to harvest offices;
Love, all alike, no season knows, nor clime,
10 Nor hours, days, months, which are the rags of time.

       Thy beams, so reverend, and strong
        Why shouldst thou think?
I could eclipse and cloud them with a wink,
But that I would not lose her sight so long:
15   If her eyes have not blinded thine,
       Look, and tomorrow late, tell me,
Whether both th'Indias of spice and mine
Be where thou left'st them, or lie here with me.
Ask for those kings whom thou saw'st yesterday,
20 And thou shalt hear, All here in one bed lay.

       She'is all states, and all princes, I,
        Nothing else is.
Princes do but play us; compared to this,
All honour's mimic; all wealth alchemy.
25   Thou sun art half as happy as we,
       In that the world's contracted thus;
Thine age asks ease, and since thy duties be
To warm the world, that's done in warming us.
Shine here to us, and thou art everywhere;
30 This bed thy centre is, these walls, thy sphere.

The Canonization

Donne ruined his chances of worldly employment and advancement by his secret, unauthorized marriage to Ann More. Does knowing this suggest a motivation for this poem? What is the tone of the opening stanza? Is it maintained throughout the poem?

7   *the King's real, or his stamped face* – the King's living face (at Court), or his head on a coin.

13   *forward spring* – early spring.

15   *plaguy bill* – the lists of deaths published in London during outbreaks of the plague.

17   *Litigious men* – those who go to law to solve grievances.

20   *fly* – butterfly, or moth.

21   *tapers* – candles (around which moths flutter until they are scorched).

23–4   *the phoenix riddle hath more wit/By us* – the phoenix was thought to be bisexual, therefore Donne suggests that they enable the myth to make sense, as they are one.

26   *die* – as so often, this has a double meaning, and refers to sexual orgasm as well as physical expiry.

The Canonization

For God's sake hold your tongue, and let me love,
  Or chide my palsy, or my gout,
My five grey hairs, or ruined fortune flout,
  With wealth your state, your mind with arts improve,
5   Take you a course, get you a place,
    Observe his Honour, or his Grace,
Or the King's real, or his stamped face
  Contemplate; what you will, approve,
  So you will let me love.

10 Alas, alas, who's injured by my love?
  What merchant's ships have my sighs drowned?
Who says my tears have overflowed his ground?
  When did my colds a forward spring remove?
  When did the heats which my veins fill
15   Add one man to the plaguy bill?
Soldiers find wars, and lawyers find out still
  Litigious men, which quarrels move,
  Though she and I do love.

Call us what you will, we are made such by love;
20 Call her one, me another fly,
We are tapers too, and at our own cost die,
  And we in us find the eagle and the dove;
    The phoenix riddle hath more wit
    By us; we two being one, are it.
25 So, to one neutral thing both sexes fit.
  We die and rise the same, and prove
  Mysterious by this love.

We can die by it, if not live by love,
  And if unfit for tombs and hearse
30 Our legend be, it will be fit for verse;
    And if no piece of chronicle we prove,

41 *glasses* – glass vessels, used in alchemy and scientific experiments. In these lines, Donne suggests that the quintessence (or essential element) of the world's soul is held in their eyes, which, in reflecting each other, show a perfect example of everything that the world can offer.

Song (Sweetest love ...)

It has been suggested that this poem was written for his wife before Donne left her to go to the Continent in 1611.

Note how the rhyme scheme and the metre shift in the two halves of each stanza. What effect does this have on the tone in which the poem can be read?

5–8 *But since ... to die* – Donne suggests here that the best way to confront the inevitability of death is to regard such temporary partings as they are now experiencing as 'feigned', or pretended, deaths. There is a sense of facing up to the finality of death by making a joke about it.

We'll build in sonnets pretty rooms;
　　As well a well wrought urn becomes
The greatest ashes, as half-acre tombs,
35　　And by these hymns, all shall approve
　　Us canonized for love.

And thus invoke us; You whom reverend love
　　Made one another's hermitage;
You, to whom love was peace, that now is rage;
40　　Who did the whole world's soul extract, and drove,
　　Into the glasses of your eyes,
　　So made such mirrors, and such spies,
That they did all to you epitomize,
　　Countries, towns, courts: beg from above
45　　A pattern of your love!

Song

Sweetest love, I do not go,
　　For weariness of thee,
Nor in hope the world can show
　　A fitter love for me;
5　　　But since that I
Must die at last, 'tis best,
To use my self in jest
　　Thus by feigned deaths to die.

Yesternight the sun went hence,
10　　And yet is here today,
He hath no desire nor sense,
　　Nor half so short a way:
　　　Then fear not me,
But believe that I shall make
15　Speedier journeys, since I take
　　More wings and spurs than he.

23   *art and length* – we give it cunning, and allow it to increase in extent.

27   *unkindly kind* – this is an oxymoron, and draws on two definitions of 'kind', i.e. natural and benevolent.

Air and Angels

This is a complex, demanding, fascinating poem, exploring and expressing the amazement which is felt when meeting the person of one's dreams. The subtleties of argument are shifting and elusive, though their thread can be followed through the poem. Prosaic interpretation or paraphrase cannot convey its complexities: it is best to accept it as it stands, having achieved an overall understanding. Donne draws on the writings of St Thomas Aquinas, and the title and part of the argument of the poem refer to the idea that angels, which are pure spirit, must create for themselves bodies of condensed air to assume a visible form (see lines 23 and 24). Donne's poems reveal his interest in angels; they are a recurrent motif.

> Note how Donne uses contradictions and abstractions to explore the inexpressibility and wonder of love, and creates a convincing and rational argument using complex metaphysical concepts. How does the final couplet affect the reading of the poem?

6   *some lovely glorious nothing* – the poet is so dazzled by her beauty that he cannot see her clearly.

O how feeble is man's power,
   That if good fortune fall,
Cannot add another hour,
20   Nor a lost hour recall!
     But come bad chance,
And we join to it our strength,
And we teach it art and length,
   Itself o'er us to advance.

25 When thou sigh'st, thou sigh'st not wind,
    But sigh'st my soul away,
When thou weep'st, unkindly kind,
   My life's blood doth decay.
    It cannot be
30 That thou lov'st me, as thou say'st.
If in thine my life thou waste,
   Thou art the best of me.

Let not thy divining heart
   Forethink me any ill,
35 Destiny may take thy part,
    And may thy fears fulfil;
    But think that we
Are but turned aside to sleep;
They who one another keep
40   Alive, ne'er parted be.

Air and Angels

Twice or thrice had I loved thee,
Before I knew thy face or name;
So in a voice, so in a shapeless flame,
Angels affect us oft, and worshipped be;
5   Still when, to where thou wert, I came,
Some lovely glorious nothing I did see.

7–14   *But since my soul ... eye, and brow* – the soul is embodied in flesh in
        order for its possessor to live; love is born from the soul and, as it
        must not surpass its parent in ingenuity, it too must assume a body,
        so it takes that of the loved woman – the woman *is* love.

15–20   *Whilst thus ... must be sought* – the conceit here is based on ships
        and sea-faring. The idea is that love, being light (as is the air from
        which angels create their bodies) needs ballast to hold a steady
        course, but her beauty (the 'wares') is too great for mere
        admiration, and even one of her hairs is too great a burden;
        something more fitting for the task must be sought.

23–4   *Then as ... doth wear* – see above.

25   *So thy love ... sphere* – so your love may be the embodiment of my
        love.

The Anniversary

The reference to 'kings' and 'favourites' in the first line indicates a dating for
this poem of 1603 or later. If it is autobiographical and refers to Donne's
marriage, it could be earlier. However, again, the subject-matter could be
fictional.

> *Some of the language of this poem reminds the reader of* The Sun Rising,
> *but the tone is more sombre. Does the poem speak of assurance, or can
> some doubts be detected? What is the effect of the question in line 25, and
> its position in the poem?*

But since my soul, whose child love is,
Takes limbs of flesh, and else could nothing do,
  More subtle than the parent is,
10 Love must not be, but take a body too,
    And therefore what thou wert, and who,
      I bid love ask, and now
That it assume thy body, I allow,
And fix itself in thy lip, eye, and brow.

15 Whilst thus to ballast love, I thought,
And so more steadily to have gone,
With wares which would sink admiration,
I saw, I had love's pinnace overfraught,
  Every thy hair for love to work upon
20 Is much too much, some fitter must be sought;
    For, nor in nothing, nor in things
Extreme, and scatt'ring bright, can love inhere;
    Then as an angel, face, and wings
Of air, nor pure as it, yet pure doth wear,
25   So thy love may be my love's sphere;
      Just such disparity
As is 'twixt air and angels' purity
'Twixt women's love, and men's will ever be.

The Anniversary

    All kings, and all their favourites,
    All glory of honours, beauties, wits,
The sun itself, which makes times, as they pass,
Is elder by a year, now, than it was
5 When thou and I first one another saw:
All other things, to their destruction draw,
    Only our love hath no decay;
This, no tomorrow hath, nor yesterday,
Running it never runs from us away,
10 But truly keeps his first, last, everlasting day.

11 *corse* – corpse.

18 *inmates* – lodgers (after our deaths, our souls will be the proof that
love exclusively dwelt in them).

27 *let us refrain* – let us put aside.

Twickenham Garden

This poem resulted from Donne's relationship with Lucy, Countess of
Bedford, who was one of his patrons, though perhaps not one so generous
as he might have wished. She acquired Twickenham Park in 1607. It is
possible that the poem was written as a compliment to her, assuming the
persona of a rejected lover as a tribute to her 'truth', i.e. faithfulness to her
marriage vows. Whether the circumstances are real or imaginary, Donne's
self-focus and analysis is characteristic. In these three sombre stanzas he
makes evident his disgust with himself and his experience, and the poem can
be read as an expression of genuine feelings of distress and shame, generated
from disappointment - of whatever kind.

*How does Donne use images drawn from the garden to intensify the
impression of despair?*

4 *balms* – healing or soothing medicines or herbs.

6 *This spider love, which transubstantiates all* - transubstantiation is the
conversion of the elements of the wine and bread of the Eucharist
into the blood and body of Christ, whilst retaining their original
appearance. The spider was regarded as poisonous, either by
converting everything it ate into poison, or, if swallowed, poisoning
anyone who ate it if it was seen (see Shakespeare's *The Winter's
Tale*, II.i lines 39–45). This is an example of Donne's deliberate
blasphemy in the service of a striking conceit.

7 *manna ... gall* – manna fed the Israelites in the desert; gall is anything
bitter.

9 *paradise ... serpent* – a reference to the Garden of Eden, where the
serpent beguiled Eve and caused the Fall of Man.

Two graves must hide thine and my corse,
   If one might, death were no divorce,
Alas, as well as other princes, we,
(Who prince enough in one another be,)
15 Must leave at last in death, these eyes, and ears,
Oft fed with true oaths, and with sweet salt tears;
   But souls where nothing dwells but love
(All other thoughts being inmates) then shall prove
This, or a love increased there above,
20 When bodies to their graves, souls from their graves remove.

And then we shall be throughly blessed,
   But we no more, than all the rest.
Here upon earth, we are kings, and none but we
Can be such kings, nor of such subjects be;
25 Who is so safe as we? where none can do
Treason to us, except one of us two.
   True and false fears let us refrain,
Let us love nobly, and live, and add again
Years and years unto years, till we attain
30 To write three score: this is the second of our reign.

Twickenham Garden

Blasted with sighs, and surrounded with tears,
   Hither I come to seek the spring,
   And at mine eyes, and at mine ears,
Receive such balms, as else cure everything;
5   But O, self traitor, I do bring
The spider love, which transubstantiates all,
   And can convert manna to gall,
And that this place may thoroughly be thought
   True paradise, I have the serpent brought.

11 *benight* – create night, darkness.

17 *mandrake* – see page 10.

19 *vials* – vessels.

27 *her truth* – faithfulness to her husband, or to a rival lover.

A Valediction: of Weeping

This is a consolatory poem. Note how the conceit which is established in the first stanza (tears as coins) provides a unifying image of roundness, which runs through the whole poem, changing and shifting according to Donne's poetic needs.

3–4 *For thy face … worth* – looking at her, his tears flow. Her face is reflected in his eyes, and is thus imprinted on his tears, just as the blank of a coin is given value by the stamping of an image when it is minted.

8 *that thou* – the reflection of you.

9 *divers* – different.

10   'Twere wholesomer for me, that winter did
      Benight the glory of this place,
      And that a grave frost did forbid
    These trees to laugh, and mock me to my face,
      But that I may not this disgrace
15   Endure, nor let leave loving, Love, let me
      Some senseless piece of this place be;
    Make me a mandrake, so I may groan here,
      Or a stone fountain weeping out my year.

    Hither with crystal vials, lovers come,
20   And take my tears, which are love's wine,
    And try your mistress' tears at home,
    For all are false, that taste not just like mine;
      Alas, hearts do not in eyes shine,
    Nor can you more judge woman's thoughts by tears,
25   Than by her shadow, what she wears,
  O perverse sex, where none is true but she,
    Who's therefore true, because her truth kills me.

A Valediction: of Weeping

    Let me pour forth
  My tears before thy face, whilst I stay here,
  For thy face coins them, and thy stamp they bear,
  And by this mintage they are something worth,
5   For thus they be
    Pregnant of thee;
  Fruits of much grief they are, emblems of more,
  When a tear falls, that thou falls which it bore,
  So thou and I are nothing then, when on a divers shore.

17–18   *Till thy tears … dissolved so* – their tears will create a flood which
         will overwhelm the world, which is his heaven as she is there.

19   *moon* – the waxing and waning of the moon controls the tides.

A Nocturnal upon St Lucy's Day, being the shortest day

Many commentators have linked this poem with Lucy, Countess of Bedford,
or with Donne's wife. If there is a real, rather than imagined, subject, it is
likely to be Ann, who died giving birth to their twelfth child, in August 1617.
(The Countess did not die until 1627.) St Lucy's Day is 13 December, which,
before the reform of the calendar in 1752, was thought to be the shortest
day.

Consider the appropriateness of the setting of the poem to its subject-matter.

3   *flasks* – powder-flasks, used to store gunpowder. The reference is
     to the stars, which were thought to store light from the sun.
     'Squibs', in the following line, are the intermittent sparks from
     spluttering grains of gunpowder.

6   *The general balm … hath drunk* – the earth is crazed with thirst, like
     one suffering from dropsy, and has soaked up the balm, the vital
     essence which maintains life.

7   *bed's-feet* – the foot of the bed. Here, Donne reverses the
     traditional belief that, when the body dies, the process begins in the
     feet.

10   On a round ball
A workman that hath copies by, can lay
An Europe, Africa, and an Asia,
And quickly make that, which was nothing, all,
    So doth each tear,
15   Which thee doth wear,
A globe, yea world by that impression grow,
Till thy tears mixed with mine do overflow
This world, by waters sent from thee, my heaven dissolved so.

    O more than moon,
20 Draw not up seas to drown me in thy sphere,
Weep me not dead, in thine arms, but forbear
To teach the sea, what it may do too soon;
    Let not the wind
    Example find,
25 To do me more harm, than it purposeth;
Since thou and I sigh one another's breath,
Whoe'er sighs most, is cruellest, and hastes the other's death.

A Nocturnal upon St Lucy's Day, being the shortest day

'Tis the year's midnight, and it is the day's,
Lucy's, who scarce seven hours herself unmasks,
    The sun is spent, and now his flasks
    Send forth light squibs, no constant rays;
5   The world's whole sap is sunk:
The general balm th'hydroptic earth hath drunk,
Whither, as to the bed's-feet, life is shrunk,
Dead and interred; yet all these seem to laugh,
Compared with me, who am their epitaph.

10 Study me then, you who shall lovers be
At the next world, that is, at the next spring:
    For I am every dead thing,

13–15   *new alchemy ... nothingness* – in alchemy, the elixir (quintessence) of a substance is isolated and extracted. Here, the process is 'new' as it extracts (expresses) this from 'nothingness'. In ancient philosophy, the quintessence was the fifth and celestial element, which is essential to all living things.

16   *privations* – deprivation.

21   *limbeck* – the vessel in which the alchemical process takes place.

25–6   *two chaoses ... aught else* – when they were concerned with anything other than themselves, they created individual states of chaos, the formlessness which was supposed to have existed before the creation of the universe.

32–4   *If I were ... properties invest* – Donne catalogues the orders of existence below the state of man, animals, plants and minerals. The idea that all things, even stones, possess some emotion derives from the writings of Pliny, a Roman author.

35   *ordinary nothing* – this assumes the absence of something. The poet's condition is the purest state, deriving from absolute nothingness.

37   *nor will my sun renew* – there are two possible readings: his vital spirits will not revive, or the woman will not return to life. Perhaps both were intended.

39   *the Goat* – the sun enters the house of Capricorn (the Goat) on 21 December; the goat is traditionally seen as an image of lust.

42–5   *Since she ... midnight is* – the 'she' in these lines could be either St Lucy, or the dead woman. It is not necessary to unravel the ambiguity, as the conceit of devotional preparation for the ritual of the festival is equally valid for either subject.

In whom love wrought new alchemy,
　　For his art did express
15　A quintessence even from nothingness,
　　From dull privations, and lean emptiness
　　He ruined me, and I am re-begot
　　Of absence, darkness, death; things which are not.

　　All others, from all things, draw all that's good,
20　Life, soul, form, spirit, whence they being have;
　　　I, by love's limbeck, am the grave
　　　Of all, that's nothing. Oft a flood
　　　　Have we two wept, and so
　　Drowned the whole world, us two; oft did we grow
25　To be two chaoses, when we did show
　　Care to aught else; and often absences
　　Withdrew our souls, and made us carcases.

　　But I am by her death (which word wrongs her)
　　Of the first nothing, the elixir grown;
30　　Were I a man, that I were one,
　　　I needs must know; I should prefer,
　　　　If I were any beast,
　　Some ends, some means; yea plants, yea stones detest,
　　And love; all, all some properties invest;
35　If I an ordinary nothing were,
　　As shadow, a light, and body must be here.

　　But I am none; nor will my sun renew.
　　You lovers, for whose sake, the lesser sun
　　　At this time to the Goat is run
40　　To fetch new lust, and give it you,
　　　　Enjoy your summer all;
　　Since she enjoys her long night's festival,
　　Let me prepare towards her, and let me call
　　This hour her vigil, and her eve, since this
45　Both the year's, and the day's deep midnight is.

A Valediction: forbidding Mourning

This poem of comfort on parting contains one of the most famous (and over-quoted) of Donne's conceits, the 'stiff twin compasses', in line 26. It is, however, only one in a series of conceits which develop the argument that constancy and unity give the assurance which binds the parted lovers, and will reunite them.

How does the opening stanza prepare the reader for the rest of the poem?

7   *profanation* – blasphemy.

8   *laity* – those who are not in the priesthood. The idea is that their love is a holy mystery which must not be revealed to the uninitiated.

9   *Moving of th'earth* – earthquakes, thought to portend disaster.

11   *trepidation of the spheres* – Donne draws his images here from a geocentric concept of the universe. 'Trepidation' is the astrological term which refers to the oscillation of the ninth sphere, which imparts movement to the other spheres. This, though much greater and grander than a mere earthquake, is benign.

13   *sublunary* – beneath the moon. It was believed that everything below the sphere of the moon is subject to change and decay, whilst everything above it is immortal.

16   *elemented it* – created its essence.

17   *refined* – reduced to essential purity.

24   *gold to airy thinness beat* – gold is the softest metal, and can be beaten nearly into transparency.

A Valediction: forbidding Mourning

As virtuous men pass mildly away,
    And whisper to their souls, to go,
Whilst some of their sad friends do say,
    The breath goes now, and some say, no:

5 So let us melt, and make no noise,
    No tear-floods, nor sigh-tempests move,
'Twere profanation of our joys
    To tell the laity our love.

Moving of th'earth brings harms and fears,
10   Men reckon what it did and meant,
But trepidation of the spheres,
    Though greater far, is innocent.

Dull sublunary lovers' love
    (Whose soul is sense) cannot admit
15 Absence, because it doth remove
    Those things which elemented it.

But we by a love, so much refined,
    That ourselves know not what it is,
Inter-assured of the mind,
20   Care less, eyes, lips, and hands to miss.

Our two souls therefore, which are one,
    Though I must go, endure not yet
A breach, but an expansion,
    Like gold to airy thinness beat.

25 If they be two, they are two so
    As stiff twin compasses are two,
Thy soul the fixed foot, makes no show
    To move, but doth, if th'other do.

34   *obliquely* – at an angle.

The Funeral

This poem, and the next one, are based on similar subject-matter. Both poems seem to combine what can be read as sincerity with defiant levity. In both, there is evidence of the influence of Donne's early Catholicism.

How do The Funeral *and* The Relic *differ in tone?*

3   *subtle* – mysterious (see 1.4).

6   *viceroy* – one who rules over a colony or tributary nation on behalf of a monarch.

9   *sinewy thread* – the nerves.

19 *idolatry* – the worship of idols, relics, or any object believed sacred.

And though it in the centre sit,
30   Yet when the other far doth roam,
It leans, and hearkens after it,
        And grows erect, as that comes home.

Such wilt thou be to me, who must
    Like th'other foot, obliquely run;
35 Thy firmness makes my circle just,
        And makes me end, where I begun.

The Funeral

Whoever comes to shroud me, do not harm
        Nor question much
That subtle wreath of hair, which crowns my arm;
The mystery, the sign you must not touch,
5   For 'tis my outward soul,
Viceroy to that, which then to heaven being gone,
        Will leave this to control,
And keep these limbs, her provinces, from dissolution.

For if the sinewy thread my brain lets fall
10   Through every part,
Can tie those parts, and make me one of all;
These hairs which upward grew, and strength and art
        Have from a better brain,
Can better do it; except she meant that I
15   By this should know my pain,
As prisoners then are manacled, when they are condemned to die.

What'er she meant by it, bury it with me,
        For since I am
Love's martyr, it might breed idolatry,
20 If into others' hands these relics came;
        As 'twas humility

23 *bravery* – defiance.

The Relic

1–2 *When my grave ... some other guest* – it was commonplace in Donne's time to re-use old graves.

3 *woman-head* – a play on the idea of maidenhead, or virginity: a woman is (presumably) no longer a virgin.

6 *bright hair* – Mary Magdalen (see 1.17) was usually depicted as having golden hair.

10 *busy day* – the Day of Judgement.

13 *mis-devotion* – implies idolatry and superstition.

17–18 *and I/A something else* – the almost coy indirectness indicates that Donne is drawing on the tradition linking Mary Magdalen and Christ as lovers. The fact that Christ's body did not remain in the grave is irrelevant in the context of the poem.

26 *guardian angels* – angels lack sexual characteristics.
27–8 *Coming ... meals* – this refers to the social convention of kissing on meeting or parting.

To afford to it all that a soul can do,
    So, 'tis some bravery,
That since you would save none of me, I bury some of you.

The Relic

When my grave is broke up again
Some second guest to entertain,
(For graves have learned that woman-head
To be to more than one a bed)
5   And he that digs it, spies
A bracelet of bright hair about the bone,
        Will he not let us alone,
And think that there a loving couple lies,
Who thought that this device might be some way
10 To make their souls, at the last busy day,
Meet at this grave, and make a little stay?

If this fall in a time, or land,
Where mis-devotion doth command,
Then, he that digs us up, will bring
15 Us, to the Bishop, and the King,
        To make us relics; then
Thou shalt be a Mary Magdalen, and I
        A something else thereby;
All women shall adore us, and some men;
20 And since at such time, miracles are sought,
I would have that age by this paper taught
What miracles we harmless lovers wrought.

First, we loved well and faithfully,
Yet knew not what we loved, nor why,
25 Difference of sex no more we knew,
    Than our guardian angels do;
        Coming and going, we

29 *Our hands ne'er touched the seals* – they remained sexually chaste.
30 *nature ... law* – love is natural; the laws of marriage are a modern restriction on its freedom.

The Prohibition

This poem takes the form of a reasoned discourse, exploring and attempting to balance the extremes of love and hate.

In what way is the structure of the poem an appropriate vehicle for its argument?

3 *unthrifty* – careless.

11 *officer* – executioner.

18 *neither's office do* – cancel each other.
19 *die* – the common double meaning: have an orgasm.

22 *So shall ... triumph be* – this refers to the Roman practice of exhibiting those captured in war before killing them. If he is her 'stage', he will be the means whereby her power is demonstrated.

Perchance might kiss, but not between those meals;
  Our hands ne'er touched the seals,
30 Which nature, injured by late law, sets free:
These miracles we did; but now alas,
All measure, and all language, I should pass,
Should I tell what a miracle she was.

The Prohibition

  Take heed of loving me,
At least remember, I forbade it thee;
  Not that I shall repair my unthrifty waste
Of breath and blood, upon thy sighs, and tears,
5   By being to thee then what to me thou wast;
But, so great joy, our life at once outwears,
    Then, lest thy love, by my death, frustrate be,
    If thou love me, take heed of loving me.

  Take heed of hating me,
10 Or too much triumph in the victory.
  Not that I shall be mine own officer,
And hate with hate again retaliate;
  But thou wilt lose the style of conqueror,
If I, thy conquest, perish by thy hate.
15   Then, lest my being nothing lessen thee,
    If thou hate me, take heed of hating me.

  Yet, love and hate me too,
So, these extremes shall neither's office do;
  Love me, that I may die the gentler way;
20 Hate me, because thy love's too great for me;
  Or let these two, themselves, nor me decay;
So I shall live thy stage, not triumph be;
    Lest thou thy love and hate and me undo,
    To let me live, Oh love and hate me too.

The Expiration

This poem was printed in 1609, with music, in a book of airs. Would it lose, or gain, anything when set to music?

    4   *benight* – turn into night.

Holy Sonnets

The following sonnets are a selection from those which Donne wrote at different periods of his life. Most of them pre-date his entry into the Church (1615). It has been suggested that some were written for the Countess of Bedford who, though a prominent member of the Jacobean court, was a devout Calvinist. Though Donne himself did not embrace that doctrine, some of its aspects (despair, fear of damnation, the concept of God's election of certain souls) underlie the argument of many of these sonnets. The first three printed here were possibly written in 1609, and may have been from the set of six sent to the Earl of Dorset.

The sonnet form is Petrarchan, in which the structure is based on an octave and sestet. The Petrarchan sestet can vary in its rhyme scheme; in these sonnets, Donne always concludes with a rhyming couplet.

Note the ways in which Donne uses the sonnet form as a vehicle for debate or exploration of an idea. How does it enable him to structure argument?

This is my play's ...

    7   *But my ... that face* – some manuscripts give an alternative reading of this line: 'Or presently, I know not, see that face'. This implies that, rather than being transported immediately after death to heaven or hell, the soul remains within the body until the Last Judgement.

  13   *Impute me righteous* – this is Protestant doctrine, whereby the soul can only saved through the righteousness of Christ conferred upon it; this makes it an elected soul. No human soul is righteous enough on its own merits.

  14   *the world, the flesh, the devil* – these words appear in the service of Holy Baptism.

The Expiration

So, so, break off this last lamenting kiss,
  Which sucks two souls, and vapours both away,
Turn thou ghost that way, and let me turn this,
  And let ourselves benight our happiest day,
5 We asked none leave to love; nor will we owe
  Any, so cheap a death, as saying, Go;

Go: and if that word have not quite killed thee,
  Ease me with death, by bidding me go too.
Oh, if it have, let my word work on me,
10   And a just office on a murderer do,
Except it be too late, to kill me so,
  Being double dead, going, and bidding, go.

Holy Sonnets

This is my play's last scene, here heavens appoint
My pilgrimage's last mile; and my race
Idly, yet quickly run, hath this last pace,
My span's last inch, my minute's latest point,
5 And gluttonous death will instantly unjoint
My body, and soul, and I shall sleep a space,
But my' ever-waking part shall see that face,
Whose fear already shakes my every joint:
Then, as my soul, to'heaven her first seat, takes flight,
10 And earth-born body, in the earth shall dwell,
So, fall my sins, that all may have their right,
To where they'are bred, and would press me, to hell.
Impute me righteous, thus purged of evil,
For thus I leave the world, the flesh, the devil.

At the round earth's ...

    1 *imagined corners* – Donne uses the image from Revelation 7: 'I saw four angels standing on the four corners of the earth ...'.

    7 *you whose eyes* – i.e. those who are still alive on the Day of Judgement.

  14 *As if thou ... blood* – the tone of doubt at the beginning of the line suggests the thought that the poet is so sinful that Christ's universal redemption cannot apply to him.

Death be not proud ...

    5 *picture* – rest and sleep are imitations of death.

  11 *poppy* – opium.

  14 *Death thou shalt die* – 1 Corinthians 15: 'The last enemy which shall be destroyed is death.'

At the round earth's imagined corners, blow
Your trumpets, angels, and arise, arise
From death, you numberless infinities
Of souls, and to your scattered bodies go,
5   All whom the flood did, and fire shall o'erthrow,
All whom war, dearth, age, agues, tyrannies,
Despair, law, chance, hath slain, and you whose eyes,
Shall behold God, and never taste death's woe,
But let them sleep, Lord, and me mourn a space,
10 For, if above all these, my sins abound,
'Tis late to ask abundance of thy grace,
When we are there; here on this lowly ground,
Teach me how to repent; for that's as good
As if thou'hadst sealed my pardon, with thy blood.

Death be not proud, though some have called thee
Mighty and dreadful, for, thou art not so,
For, those, whom thou think'st, thou dost overthrow,
Die not, poor death, nor yet canst thou kill me;
5   From rest and sleep, which but thy pictures be,
Much pleasure, then from thee, much more must flow,
And soonest our best men with thee do go,
Rest of their bones, and soul's delivery.
Thou art slave to fate, chance, kings, and desperate men,
10 And dost with poison, war, and sickness dwell,
And poppy, or charms can make us sleep us well,
And better than thy stroke; why swell'st thou then?
One short sleep past, we wake eternally,
And death shall be no more, Death thou shalt die.

What if this present ...

    2   *Mark ... –* an exhortation to contemplation.

  10 *profane mistresses –* as opposed to sacred; erotic imagery in religious writing is not uncommon.

11–12 *Beauty ... sign of rigour –* Donne refers to his experiences with women here, stating that those who are beautiful show compassion, whilst ugly women resist attempts at seduction. Logically, therefore, the beauty of Christ is proof of His mercy.

  14 *beauteous form –* this refers to the image of Christ.

Batter my heart ...

    5   *usurped –* seized and controlled by an enemy.

    7   *Reason your viceroy –* reason is what distinguishes man from the lower orders of creation and links him to the higher, such as angels.

What if this present were the world's last night?
Mark in my heart, O soul, where thou dost dwell,
The picture of Christ crucified, and tell
Whether that countenance can thee affright,
5 Tears in his eyes quench the amazing light,
Blood fills his frowns, which from his pierced head fell,
And can that tongue adjudge thee unto hell,
Which prayed forgiveness for his foes' fierce spite?
No, no; but as in my idolatry
10 I said to all my profane mistresses,
Beauty, of pity, foulness only is
A sign of rigour: so I say to thee,
To wicked spirits are horrid shapes assigned,
This beauteous form assures a piteous mind.

Batter my heart, three-personed God; for, you
As yet but knock, breathe, shine, and seek to mend;
That I may rise, and stand, o'erthrow me,'and bend
Your force, to break, blow, burn, and make me new.
5 I, like an usurped town, to'another due,
Labour to admit you, but oh, to no end,
Reason your viceroy in me, me should defend,
But is captived, and proves weak or untrue,
Yet dearly'I love you, and would be loved fain,
10 But am betrothed unto your enemy,
Divorce me, untie, or break that knot again,
Take me to you, imprison me, for I
Except you'enthral me, never shall be free,
Nor ever chaste, except you ravish me.

I am a little world ...

1 *little world* – the concept of the human body as microcosm, the little world, which contained all the elements of the macrocosm, the universe.

2 *angelic sprite* – see page 20.

4 *both parts* – body and soul.

6 *new spheres ... new lands* – refers to the proposition of the Primum Mobile (the 'first mover') by Ptolemy, and further spheres by later astronomers; 'new lands' probably refers to the discoveries made by Columbus, Drake, and other pioneering voyagers.

9 *drowned no more* – Genesis 9.11: '... neither shall there any more be a flood to destroy the earth.'

10 *burnt* – 2 Peter 3.12: ' ... the coming of the day of God, wherein the heavens being on fire shall be dissolved, and the elements shall melt with fervent heat.'

13–14 *And burn me ... eating heal* – Psalm 69.9: 'For the zeal of thine house hath eaten me up.'; Isaiah 9.7: 'The zeal of the Lord of Hosts will perform this.'

Since she whom I loved ...

This sonnet was written after Ann Donne's death in 1617.

2 *to hers, and my good* – her death benefits her, as she is in heaven, and Donne, because it makes him contemplate serious spiritual matters.

5 *whet* – become keen, like the sharpened edge of a knife.

8 *A holy, thirsty dropsy* – his spiritual thirst is insatiable.

12 *saints and angels* – a reminder of Donne's Roman Catholic upbringing.

14 *world, flesh, yea Devil* – see note page 40.

I am a little world made cunningly
Of elements, and an angelic sprite,
But black sin hath betrayed to endless night
My world's both parts, and, oh, both parts must die.
5   You which beyond that heaven which was most high
Have found new spheres, and of new lands can write,
Pour new seas in mine eyes, that so I might
Drown my world with my weeping earnestly,
Or wash it, if it must be drowned no more:
10   But oh it must be burnt; alas the fire
Of lust and envy have burnt it heretofore,
And made it fouler; let their flames retire,
And burn me O Lord, with a fiery zeal
Of thee and thy house, which doth in eating heal.

Since she whom I loved hath paid her last debt
To nature, and to hers, and my good is dead,
And her soul early into heaven ravished,
Wholly in heavenly things my mind is set.
5   Here the admiring her my mind did whet
To seek thee God; so streams do show the head,
But though I have found thee, and thou my thirst hast fed,
A holy thirsty dropsy melts me yet.
But why should I beg more love, when as thou
10   Dost woo my soul, for hers offering all thine:
And dost not only fear lest I allow
My love to saints and angels, things divine,
But in thy tender jealousy dost doubt
Lest the world, flesh, yea Devil put thee out.

Oh, to vex me ...

    5   *humorous* – changeable, controlled by the humours which affect his character.

   13   *ague* – fit of uncontrollable trembling.

Divine Poems

Good Friday 1613. Riding Westward

Donne rode to Montgomery, on the Welsh borders, to visit Sir Edward Herbert (the son of his benefactor Magdalen Herbert, and brother of the poet George Herbert), from Polesworth in Warwickshire, the estate of his friend and patron Sir Henry Goodyer. The poem is a meditation on the Crucifixion. The landscape through which Donne is riding plays no part in the poem. There is, however, a parallel between the steady covering of the physical ground, and the spiritual journey of the poem. Note how the pun on 'sun' underlies the structure and argument.

    1   *Let ...* – let me assume, or postulate.

  1–2   *sphere ... intelligence* – the opening conceit draws on the Platonic theory that the spheres (which were the form and structure of the Ptolemaic universe) were controlled by 'intelligences', or spirits. Donne is working on the idea that devotion is the driving force of the soul.

    4   *foreign motions* – the inner spheres were influenced by the movement of the outer spheres.

    8   *first mover* – the Primum Mobile. Its movement set all the spheres in motion. It was thought that its natural direction was west to east, but that its action was so powerful that it caused the other spheres to spin in the opposite direction, in a kind of back-wash.

   11   *sun* – sun/son is the unifying motif of the meditation.

   17   *must die* – Exodus 33.20: 'Thou canst not see my face: for there shall no man see me, and live.' (God speaking to Moses.)

Oh, to vex me, contraries meet in one:
Inconstancy unnaturally hath begot
A constant habit; that when I would not
I change in vows, and in devotion.
5   As humorous is my contrition
As my profane love, and as soon forgot:
As riddlingly distempered, cold and hot,
As praying, as mute; as infinite, as none.
I durst not view heaven yesterday; and today
10   In prayers, and flattering speeches I court God:
Tomorrow I quake with true fear of his rod.
So my devout fits come and go away
Like a fantastic ague: save that here
Those are my best days, when I shake with fear.

Good Friday, 1613. Riding Westward

Let man's soul be a sphere, and then, in this,
The intelligence that moves, devotion is,
And as the other spheres, by being grown
Subject to foreign motions, lose their own,
5   And being by others hurried every day,
Scarce in a year their natural form obey:
Pleasure or business, so, our souls admit
For their first mover, and are whirled by it.
Hence is't, that I am carried towards the west
10   This day, when my soul's form bends toward the east.
There I should see a sun, by rising set,
And by that setting endless day beget;
But that Christ on this Cross, did rise and fall,
Sin had eternally benighted all.
15   Yet dare I'almost be glad, I do not see
That spectacle of too much weight for me.
Who sees God's face, that is self life, must die;
What a death were it then to see God die?

20 *footstool crack, and the sun wink* – Isaiah 66.1: 'Thus saith the Lord ... the earth is my footstool . .'; Matthew 27.45, 51: ' ... there was darkness all over the land ... the earth did quake and the rocks rent.'

19–24 *hands which span the poles ... antipodes* – the body of Christ is described as encompassing the universe.

25–6 *that blood ... not of his* – there was a theory that the soul inhabited the blood of the human body. Mankind depends on the shedding of Christ's blood for redemption, whether or not Christ's own soul resided in His blood.

30 *miserable mother* – contemplation of Mary, the mother of Christ, is a traditional aspect of Catholic devotion. She was 'God's partner' as she bore His son.

38 *corrections* – punishment.

It made his own lieutenant Nature shrink,
20 It made his footstool crack, and the sun wink.
Could I behold those hands which span the poles,
And tune all spheres at once, pierced with those holes?
Could I behold that endless height which is
Zenith to us, and to'our antipodes,
25 Humbled below us? or that blood which is
The seat of all our souls, if not of his,
Made dirt of dust, or that flesh which was worn,
By God, for his apparel, ragged, and torn?
If on these things I durst not look, durst I
30 Upon his miserable mother cast mine eye,
Who was God's partner here, and furnished thus
Half of that sacrifice, which ransomed us?
Though these things, as I ride, be from mine eye,
They'are present yet unto my memory,
35 For that looks towards them; and thou look'st towards me,
O Saviour, as thou hang'st upon the tree;
I turn my back to thee, but to receive
Corrections, till thy mercies bid thee leave.
O think me worth thine anger, punish me,
40 Burn off my rusts, and my deformity,
Restore thine image, so much, by thy grace,
That thou mayst know me, and I'll turn my face.

A Hymn to God the Father

This poem was written in 1623, during illness. Note the recurrent pun on Donne's own name in the penultimate line of each stanza.

 1 *that sin where I begun* – original sin.

14 *I shall perish on the shore* – this refers to lack of faith in redemption, and the belief that there is no afterlife; death is final.

15 *Sun* – another pun: the Son of God brought salvation and eternal life to mankind.

A Hymn to God the Father

Wilt thou forgive that sin where I begun,
   Which is my sin, though it were done before?
Wilt thou forgive those sins through which I run,
   And do them still: though still I do deplore?
5   When thou hast done, thou hast not done,
      For, I have more.

Wilt thou forgive that sin by which I have won
   Others to sin? and, made my sin their door?
Wilt thou forgive that sin which I did shun
10   A year, or two: but wallowed in, a score?
    When thou has done, thou hast not done,
      For, I have more.

I have a sin of fear, that when I have spun
   My last thread, I shall perish on the shore;
15   Swear by thyself, that at my death thy Sun
   Shall shine as it shines now, and heretofore;
    And, having done that, thou hast done,
      I fear no more.

George Herbert (1593 – 1633)

George Herbert was born in Montgomery, on the Welsh borders, into a distinguished family, many of whose members were eminent in politics and the arts. His mother, Magdalen, was a strong personality; a pious and beautiful woman, she bore seven sons and three daughters to her husband Richard, who died when George was three years old. Magdalen Herbert moved the family to London, where she became the friend and patron of John Donne, who stayed at her house in Chelsea, and who wrote her a celebratory elegy. She married as second husband Sir John Danvers, a favourite of Francis Bacon, the Lord Chancellor. This second marriage appears to have been both harmonious and beneficial to the whole family. George Herbert grew up in a family which was in contact with those who were highest and most influential in court circles, whilst the close links with the older poet and (later) priest, John Donne, had a positive effect on his life and work.

George Herbert entered Westminster School at the age of twelve, and in 1609 he went on to Trinity College, Cambridge, where he was elected a Fellow in 1616. At this time, his ambitions appear to have been secular; he exploited his family connections to obtain the post of Public Orator. Such behaviour was standard for the time, and George Herbert was behaving just as most other young men would have done, given the opportunity. His family members were successful and well-respected; his older brother Edward (Lord Herbert of Cherbury) was Ambassador to France, and a poet, philosopher and soldier (an archetypal Renaissance man) and it is likely that George felt that his life could, given the right circumstances, follow a similar pattern. However, there was an early glimpse of another side to his character: a New Year's letter to his mother in 1610 dedicated his poetic powers to God, and enclosed two religious sonnets.

As a Fellow of Trinity College, Herbert should have taken holy orders within seven years, but, at first, he showed little inclination to do so. He spent two brief terms representing Montgomery in Parliament, then, probably about the end of 1624, he was ordained. The delay may have been due to personal doubts, and his own ill-health; his decision to enter the Church may have been the result of disillusionment with the worldly life he had followed, and influenced by John Donne. He was appointed prebendary of Leighton Bromswold, which was near Little

Gidding, where his Cambridge friend, Nicholas Ferrar, had established a religious community. George Herbert spent his own money restoring the church which had been put into his care.

Once the step into the priesthood had been taken, Herbert's life (a sadly short one) was totally dedicated to his calling, and to the active living of a Christian life. He married his stepfather's cousin, and he and his wife adopted two of their nieces, who were orphans. In April 1630 George Herbert became vicar of Bemerton, a tiny, obscure Wiltshire parish – very different from Donne's great office of Dean of St Paul's. Herbert's prose work *A Priest to The Temple, or The Country Parson*, sets 'a mark to aim at', and his clear, pragmatic yet reverent approach to the life and work of the priesthood is characteristic of the man, who was loved and held in reverence by all who knew him.

George Herbert died of consumption in 1633. Knowing that he was dying, he sent his English poems to Nicholas Ferrar, asking him to publish them in the thought they might 'turn to the advantage of any dejected soul'. This collection, **The Temple**, was published later that year, and the poems were instantly acclaimed, both for their poetic and their spiritual qualities.

All the examples we have of Herbert's poetry are religious, and his voice is a totally individual one. As an exploration and analysis of a relationship with God, they reveal a man of honesty and humility, who speaks with aristocratic courtesy in a direct, colloquial voice. As a poet, George Herbert displays complete mastery of form and expression: his verse structures are varied and inventive, created in harmony with his subjects. His voice is both intimate and dramatic, capable of exploring and explaining great and complex spiritual truths in language which communicates with clarity and freshness. One does not need to share Herbert's faith to appreciate him, both as a poet and as a man.

Herbert drew upon the structures and artefacts which surrounded him as a priest as sources for his poetic meditations. Several of his poems are based on the church building itself: the metaphysical and allegorical interrelationship between devotion and the place which has been made for it provide the sustained images. *The Church-Floor* and *The Windows* are representative of this aspect of Herbert's writing.

> *What can you deduce about Herbert's feelings about the fabric of the church from the way in which he writes?*

The Church-Floor

Each feature of the floor signifies a Christian virtue.

10 *one sure bond* – Colossians 3.14: 'And above all these things put on charity, which is the bond of perfectness.' 'Love' and 'Charity' are very closely related in Christian terminology, and the words are often used interchangeably. Paul wrote of 'faith, hope and charity' in I Corinthians 13, and modern versions of the New Testament often replace the last of these with the word 'love'. 'Caritas' (Latin) means love of one's fellow human beings.

14 *curious veins* – fine, delicate veins of different colours.

19 *the* Architect – God.

The Windows

2 *crazy* – flawed.

4 *transcendent* – above all others.

The Church-Floor

Mark you the floor? that square and speckled stone,
    Which looks so firm and strong,
        Is *Patience*:

And th' other black and grave, wherewith each one
5   Is checkered all along,
        Humility:

The gentle rising, which on either hand
    Leads to the Choir above,
        Is *Confidence*:

10 But the sweet cement, which in one sure band
    Ties the whole frame, is *Love*
        And *Charity*.

    Hither sometimes Sin steals, and stains
    The marble's neat and curious veins:
15 But all is cleansèd when the marble weeps.
    Sometimes Death, puffing at the door,
     Blows all the dust about the floor:
    But while he thinks to spoil the room, he sweeps.
     Blest be the *Architect*, whose art
20 Could build so strong in a weak heart.

The Windows

Lord, how can man preach thy eternal word?
    He is a brittle crazy glass:
Yet in thy temple thou dost him afford
    This glorious and transcendent place,
5   To be a window, through thy grace.

6 *anneal in glass thy story* – to anneal is to fix, or strengthen, by
   heating and slow cooling. Herbert refers to the biblical scenes
   which were depicted in the stained glass windows, which often
   provided subject-matter for sermons.

The church calendar, as well as the daily and weekly services, provided
Herbert the priest with a focus and structure for his life, and material for his
poetry. The three poems which follow celebrate the major festivals of the
Christian church.

> **What do these poems convey about Herbert's personal faith?**

Christmas

3 *full cry* – this term from hunting looks forward to the pun on 'dear'
   in l.5.

6 *expecting* – waiting.

6–7 *the grief/Of pleasures* – this kind of startling paradox is found
     throughout Herbert's writing: it is a technique characteristic of
     metaphysical poetry.

8 *passengers* – travellers. The extended conceit of a traveller arriving
   at an inn is inextricably linked with the theme of the poem.

14 *rack* – manger.

But when thou dost anneal in glass thy story,
      Making thy life to shine within
The holy Preacher's; then the light and glory
      More rev'rend grows, and more doth win:
10   Which else shows wat'rish, bleak, and thin.

Doctrine and life, colours and light, in one
      When they combine and mingle, bring
A strong regard and awe: but speech alone
      Doth vanish like a flaring thing,
15   And in the ear, not conscience ring.

Christmas

All after pleasures as I rid one day,
    My horse and I, both tired, body and mind,
    With full cry of affections, quite astray,
I took up in the next inn I could find.
5 There when I came, whom found I but my dear,
    My dearest Lord, expecting till the grief
    Of pleasures brought me to him, ready there
To be all passengers' most sweet relief?
O Thou, whose glorious, yet contracted light,
10   Wrapt in night's mantle, stole into a manger;
    Since my dark soul and brutish is thy right
To Man of all beasts be not thou a stranger:
    Furnish and deck my soul, that thou mayst have
    A better lodging than a rack or grave.

15 The shepherds sing; and shall I silent be?
    My God, no hymn for thee?
My soul's a shepherd too; a flock it feeds
    Of thoughts, and words, and deeds.
The pasture is thy word: the streams, thy grace
20   Enriching all the place.

26   *Himself the candle hold* – Proverbs 20.27: 'The spirit of man is the candle of the Lord.'

Good Friday

It is possible that the last three stanzas of this poem were intended to stand separately, as in one early edition they are entitled *The Passion*. In another edition, they begin a new page after the first four stanzas, under the title *Good Friday*.

4   *tell* – count.

8   *all* – i.e all the stars.

11–12   *be sign/Of the true vine?* – signify the true vine. John 15.1: 'I am the true vine …'

Shepherd and flock shall sing, and all my powers
    Out-sing the day-light hours.
Then we will chide the sun for letting night
    Take up his place and right:
25 We sing one common Lord; wherefore he should
    Himself the candle hold.
I will go searching, till I find a sun
    Shall stay, till we have done;
A willing shiner, that shall shine as gladly,
30   As frost-nipt suns look sadly.
Then we will sing, and shine all our own day,
    And one another pay:
His beams shall cheer my breast, and both so twine,
Till ev'n his beams sing, and my music shine.

Good Friday

    O my chief good,
How shall I measure out thy blood?
How shall I count what thee befell,
    And each grief tell?

5   Shall I thy woes
Number according to thy foes?
Or, since one star showed thy first breath,
    Shall all thy death?

    Or shall each leaf,
10 Which falls in Autumn, score a grief?
Or cannot leaves, but fruit, be sign
    Of the true vine?

    Then let each hour
Of my whole life one grief devour;
15 That thy distress through all may run,
    And be my sun.

18 *several sins* – each separate sin.

    get – beget, conceive.

19 *each beast his cure doth know* – this refers to the country belief that
    an animal can find the herb which will cure its sickness (a belief
    which has much validity!).

Easter

As with *Good Friday*, one edition offers the last three stanzas (in a slightly
different version) as a separate poem. However, most recent editors agree
that these are the 'song' announced in stanza 3. Herbert's poetic forms were
innovative, and he used verse with a freedom which allowed him to match
form with substance; this poem seems to exemplify this aspect of his writing.

 5 *calcined* – consumed with fire. The idea is that the impurities are
    burned away, leaving only the finest element. In alchemaic
    practices, gold was regarded as the purest of all materials.

Or rather let
My several sins their sorrows get;
That as each beast his cure doth know,
20   Each sin may so.

Since blood is fittest, Lord, to write
Thy sorrows in, and bloody fight;
My heart hath store, write there, where in
One box doth lie both ink and sin:

25   And when sin spies so many foes,
Thy whips, thy nails, thy wounds, thy woes,
All come to lodge there, sin may say,
No room for me, and fly away.

Sin being gone, oh fill the place
30   And keep possession with thy grace;
Let sin take courage and return,
And all the writings blot or burn.

Easter

Rise heart; thy Lord is risen. Sing his praise
        Without delays,
Who takes thee by the hand, that thou likewise
        With him mayst rise:
5 That, as his death calcinèd thee to dust,
His life may make thee gold, and much more, just.

Awake, my lute, and struggle for thy part
        With all thy art.
The cross taught all wood to resound his name,
10   Who bore the same.
His stretchèd sinews taught all strings, what key
Is best to celebrate this most high day.

13   *consort* – harmonize.

     twist – intertwine the various melodic strands.

15   *three parts vied* – the three tones of a chord blend with each other.

19   *straw* – strew.

22   *sweets* – perfumes: possibly a reference to the sweet oils used to anoint a corpse.

29   *miss* – count erroneously.

In the following three poems, Herbert examines aspects of his work: *Jordan (I)* and *Jordan (II)* are concerned with the making of poetry, and *Aaron* examines the role of priest. The river Jordan was where Christ was baptized: its use as title by Herbert indicates his dedication of his poetic talent to Christian service, as opposed to secular. (The classical source of poetry was the springs of Mount Helicon, the home of the Muses.)

What do these poems convey about Herbert's attitude to his two callings?

Jordan (I)

1   *false hair* – the reference is to the custom of wearing wigs or hairpieces to enhance personal appearance: the implication is of artificiality.

5   *painted chair* – in Plato's *Republic*, the philosopher Socrates is quoted as attacking imitative art, suggesting that a painting of a couch is twice removed from reality, as the object which it depicts is itself an imitation of the purest form, i.e. the idea of a couch. This concept is reiterated at the end of the second stanza.

9   *divines* – understands, interprets.

11   *shepherds* – the image of poet as shepherd has a long tradition.

12   *who list* – whoever wishes (to).

     pull for prime – primero was a card-game, a precursor of the modern game of poker: the expression means 'to gain a winning hand'.

Consort both heart and lute, and twist a song
Pleasant and long:
15 Or since all music is but three parts vied
And multiplied,
O let thy blessèd Spirit bear a part,
And make up our defects with his sweet art.

I got me flowers to straw thy way;
20 I got me boughs off many a tree:
But though wast up by break of day,
And broughtst thy sweets along with thee.

The sun arising in the East,
Though he give light, and th' East perfume;
25 If they should offer to contest
With thy arising, they presume.

Can there be any day but this,
Though many suns to shine endeavour?
We count three hundred, but we miss:
30 There is but one, and that one ever.

Jordan (I)

Who says that fictions only and false hair
Become a verse? Is there in truth no beauty?
Is all good structure in a winding stair?
May no lines pass, except they do their duty
5   Not to a true, but painted chair?

It is no verse, except enchanted groves
And sudden arbours shadow coarse-spun lines?
Must purling streams refresh a lover's loves?
Must all be veiled, while he that reads, divines,
10   Catching the sense at two removes?

Shepherds are honest people; let them sing:
Riddle who list, for me, and pull for prime:
I envy no man's nightingale or spring;
Nor let them punish me with loss of rhyme,
15   Who plainly say, *My God, My King*.

Jordan (II)

3   *quaint words* – elaborate, artificial words.

    trim invention – the reference is to rhetorical theory, the aspect of writing in which the subject-matter is developed.

8   *sped* – successful.

10 *quick* – alive.

15 *a friend* – Herbert's 'friend', in this poem and elsewhere, is Christ. In John 15, Christ is shown as speaking of love and friendship, stating specifically 'Ye are my friends …'.

16 *wide* – as in 'wide of the mark', i.e. missing its target.

Aaron

Aaron was the brother of Moses, and one of the first priests of the Israelites. In Exodus 28, there is a description of the garments which he wore, which consecrated him to minister in the office of priest. This is too long to quote extensively here, but reference to it provides interesting background to this poem.

2   *light and perfections* – 'And thou shalt put in the breastplate of judgement the Urim and Thummim; and they shall be upon Aaron's heart when he goeth in before the Lord …'. Urim and Thummim were sacred stones.

Jordan (II)

When first my lines of heav'nly joys made mention,
Such was their lustre, they did so excel,
That I sought out quaint words, and trim invention;
My thoughts began to burnish, sprout, and swell,
5   Curling with metaphors a plain intention,
Decking the sense, as if it were to sell.

Thousands of notions in my brain did run,
Off'ring their service, if I were not sped:
I often blotted what I had begun;
10   This was not quick enough, and that was dead.
Nothing could seem too rich to clothe the sun,
Much less those joys which trample on his head.

As flames do work and wind, when they ascend,
So did I weave my self into the sense.
15   But while I bustled, I might hear a friend
Whisper, *How wide is all this long pretence!*
There is in love a sweetness ready penned:
Copy out only that, and save expense.

Aaron

Holiness on the head,
    Light and perfections on the breast,
Harmonious bells below, raising the dead
    To lead them unto life and rest:
5   Thus are true Aarons drest.

Profaneness in my head,
    Defects and darkness in my breast,
A noise of passions ringing me for dead
    Unto a place where is no rest:
10   Poor priest thus am I drest.

19–20   *the old man ... new drest* – the sinful person is redeemed through
        the righteousness and sacrifice of Christ.

The following selection is drawn from those poems which deal with different
aspects of human life and experience, the relationship between man and
God, Christian life and practices.

Prayer (I)

*The poem is constructed on a series of analogues for its subject. Which of
these images appeal to you most strongly, and why?*

1   *banquet* – in Herbert's time, this term was applied to a separate
     course, such as a dessert, of sweetmeats, fruits and wine. The
     modern meaning is not inappropriate, however.

     angels' age – angels are ageless, so the implication is eternity,
     timelessness.

2   *God's breath* – God breathed life into Adam, the first man.

3   *soul in paraphrase* – a paraphrase extracts the fundamental meaning
     of a passage of writing, therefore the essence of the soul is implied
     here.

4   *plummet* – a plumb-, or sounding-line, which tests vertical distances.

5   *engine* – a war-machine, such as a catapult.

     sinners' tower – i.e. to ascend to God.

7   *transposing* – as in music, changing key.

10   *manna* – the food of the Israelites in the desert.

11   *ordinary* – implies something that is regular, experienced on a daily
     basis, such as a meal.

     man well drest – see *Aaron* for another use of this concept by
     Herbert.

Only another head
I have, another heart and breast,
Another music, making live not dead,
Without whom I could have no rest:
15   In him I am well drest.

Christ is my only head,
My alone only heart and breast,
My only music, striking me ev'n dead;
That to the old man I may rest,
20   And be in him new drest.

So holy in my head,
Perfect and light in my dear breast,
My doctrine tuned by Christ (who is not dead,
But lives in me while I do rest):
25   Come people; Aaron's drest.

Prayer (I)

Prayer the Church's banquet, angels' age,
    God's breath in man returning to his birth,
    The soul in paraphrase, heart in pilgrimage,
    The Christian plummet sounding heav'n and earth;
5 Engine against th' Almighty, sinners' tower,
    Reversèd thunder, Christ-side-piercing spear,
    The six-day's world transposing in an hour,
A kind of tune, which all things hear and fear;
Softness, and peace, and joy, and love, and bliss,
10   Exalted manna, gladness of the best,
    Heaven in ordinary, man well drest,
The milky way, the bird of Paradise,
    Church-bells beyond the stars heard, the soul's
      blood,
    The land of spices; something understood.

The Pearl. Matth. 13.45

The reference is to a passage concerning Christ's preaching: '... the kingdom of heaven is like unto a merchant man, seeking goodly pearls: who, when he had found one pearl of great price, went and sold all that he had, and bought it.'

What does this poem tell you about Herbert's own background and experiences in the secular world?

1–2   *the head/And pipes* – Herbert conflates images based on an olive press and a printing press.

5   *conspire* – unite to produce an effect on earthly things.

6   *forced by fire* – tortured.

12   *wit* – intelligence; lively, inventive expression.

13   *vies* – contests.

18   *spirit* – liquor.

22   *relishes* – pleasures, and, in music, elaborate phrasing.

26   *unbridled store* – wild abundance.

27   *my stuff is flesh* – he is human, and therefore subject to natural desires.

The Pearl

MATTH. 13. 45

> I know the ways of Learning; both the head
> And pipes that feed the press, and make it run;
> What reason hath from nature borrowèd,
> Or of itself, like a good huswife, spun
> 5 In laws and policy; what the stars conspire,
> What willing nature speaks, what forced by fire;
> Both th' old discoveries, and the new-found seas,
> The stock and surplus, cause and history:
> All these stand open, or I have the keys:
> 10   Yet I love thee.
>
> I know the ways of Honour, what maintains
> The quick returns of courtesy and wit:
> In vies of favours whether party gains,
> When glory swells the heart, and moldeth it
> 15 To all expressions both of hand and eye,
> Which on the world a true-love-knot may tie,
> And bear the bundle, wheresoe'er it goes:
> How many drams of spirit there must be
> To sell my life unto my friends or foes:
> 20   Yet I love thee.
>
> I know the ways of Pleasure, the sweet strains,
> The lullings and the relishes of it;
> The propositions of hot blood and brains;
> What mirth and music mean; what love and wit
> 25 Have done these twenty hundred years, and more:
> I know the projects of unbridled store:
> My stuff is flesh, not brass; my senses live,
> And grumble oft, that they have more in me
> Than he that curbs them, being but one to five:
> 30   Yet I love thee.

32 *sealed* – to 'seel' a hawk's eyelids is to sew them together, a technique once used to train hawks to return to the hand.

34 *commodities* – material advantages.

38 *silk twist* – in Homer's *Iliad*, Zeus joins heaven and earth with a gold chain. This is an example of a subtle echo of Herbert's own classical 'Learning'.

Man

In this poem, Herbert draws on the concept of microcosm (the little world of the human body) and macrocosm (the universe). This provides him with a rich source of metaphysical conceits, as it did other poets. In stanza 8, the comprehensive vision of the world and the idea of man's unconcerned destruction of other living things on this planet seems as much in keeping with twentieth-century concepts (generally understood to have been influenced by Eastern philosophies such as Buddhism and Jainism) as with seventeenth-century Christianity.

What image of man is created here, and why does Herbert show him as so splendid?

5 *to* – i.e. compared to.

12 *upon the score* – they should be part of the reckoning, and to our credit, not theirs.

I know all these, and have them in my hand:
Therefore not sealèd, but with open eyes
I fly to thee, and fully understand
Both the main sale, and the commodities;
35 And at what rate and price I have thy love;
With all the circumstances that may move:
Yet through these labyrinths, not my groveling wit,
But thy silk twist let down from heav'n to me,
Did both conduct and teach me, how by it
40   To climb to thee.

Man

My God, I heard this day,
That none doth build a stately habitation,
   But he that means to dwell therein.
   What house more stately hath there been,
5 Or can be, than is Man? to whose creation
   All things are in decay.

For Man is ev'ry thing,
And more: He is a tree, yet bears more fruit;
   A beast, yet is, or should be more:
10   Reason and speech we only bring.
Parrots may thank us, if they are not mute,
   They go upon the score.

Man is all symmetry,
Full of proportions, one limb to another,
15   And all to all the world besides:
   Each part may call the furthest, brother:
For head with foot hath private amity,
   And both with moons and tides.

21   *dismount* – bring down: as man sees the star, so it is brought into his personal sphere.

34   *kind* – natural, having kinship with man: however, there are implications of the modern meaning of this word.

38–9   *Waters … Distinguished, our habitation* – the waters were set apart, or divided, to provide man's place on earth.

40   *our meat* – again, the subject of the line is 'waters': they feed man when falling as rain.

42   *neat* – well-ordered.

Nothing hath got so far,
20 But Man hath caught and kept it, as his prey.
His eyes dismount the highest star:
He is in little all the sphere.
Herbs gladly cure our flesh; because that they
Find their acquaintance there.

25 For us the winds do blow,
The earth doth rest, heav'n move, and fountains flow.
Nothing we see, but means our good,
As our delight, or as our treasure:
The whole is, either our cupboard of food,
30 Or cabinet of pleasure.

The stars have us to bed;
Night draws the curtain, which the sun withdraws;
Music and light attend our head.
All things unto our flesh are kind
35 In their descent and being; to our mind
In their ascent and cause.

Each thing is full of duty:
Waters united are our navigation;
Distinguishèd, our habitation;
40 Below, our drink; above, our meat;
Both are our cleanliness. Hath one such beauty?
Then how are all things neat?

More servants wait on Man,
Than he'll take notice of: in ev'ry path
45 He treads down that which doth befriend him,
When sickness makes him pale and wan.
Oh mighty love! Man is one world, and hath
Another to attend him.

52 *wit* – intelligence, wisdom.

Life

In this poem, Herbert writes of the brevity of human life, and his acceptance of the inevitability of death.

How do you react to lines 11 and 12? How do they interact with the rest of the poem?

1 *posy* – of flowers, but the term can also be applied to poetry.
3 *band* – i.e. the band which ties the flowers together and, by analogy, within the bounds of the poem: a metaphysical linking of process and product.

12 *sug'ring* – sweetening, making palatable.

Since then, my God, thou hast
50 So brave a palace built; O dwell in it,
    That it may dwell with thee at last!
    Till then, afford us so much wit;
That, as the world serves us, we may serve thee,
    And both thy servants be.

Life

I made a posy, while the day ran by:
Here will I smell my remnant out, and tie
    My life within this band.
But Time did beckon to the flowers, and they
5 By noon most cunningly did steal away,
    And withered in my hand.

My hand was next to them, and then my heart:
I took, without more thinking, in good part
    Time's gentle admonition:
10 Who did so sweetly death's sad taste convey,
Making my mind to smell my fatal day;
    Yet sug'ring the suspicion.

Farewell dear flowers, sweetly your time ye spent,
Fit, while ye lived, for smell or ornament,
15   And after death for cures.
I follow straight without complaints or grief,
Since if my scent be good, I care not, if
    It be as short as yours.

Mortification

A poem in the 'memento mori' tradition: thoughts of death provide material for meditative reflection. The twentieth-century playwright, Samuel Beckett, wrote 'they give birth astride of a grave': the tradition is timeless.

> *Do you find this a pessimistic poem?*

2   *sweets* – perfumes.

5   *clouts* – swaddling clothes, the first clothing of a new-born baby.
    winding-sheets – the cloths in which a corpse is wrapped.

13   *frank and free* – without obligations, and able to indulge personal desires.

17   *knell* – the passing-bell, rung whilst a person is dying, and afterwards to mark the death.

18   *which shall befriend him* – i.e. those friends who will comfort him whilst he is dying.

24   *attends* – awaits.

29   *litter* – a portable bed.
    bier – a moveable frame which supports a coffin.

Mortification

How soon doth man decay!
When clothes are taken from a chest of sweets
   To swaddle infants, whose young breath
     Scarce knows the way;
5   Those clouts are little winding sheets,
Which do consign and send them unto death.

When boys go first to bed,
They step into their voluntary graves,
   Sleep binds them fast; only their breath
10   Makes them not dead:
   Successive nights like rolling waves,
Convey them quickly, who are bound for death.

When youth is frank and free,
And calls for music, while his veins do swell,
15   All day exchanging mirth and breath
     In company;
   That music summons to the knell,
Which shall befriend him at the hour of death.

When man grows staid and wise,
20 Getting a house and home, where he may move
   Within the circle of his breath,
    Schooling his eyes;
   That dumb inclosure maketh love
Unto the coffin, that attends his death.

25   When age grows low and weak,
Marking his grave, and thawing ev'ry year,
   Till all do melt, and drown his breath
    When he would speak;
   A chair or litter shows the bier,
30 Which shall convey him to the house of death.

32   *solemnity* – solemn ritual.

33   *hearse* – not the modern meaning of a vehicle which transports the coffin, but a covering for the coffin, a framework on which tributes to the dead person were placed.

The Pulley

This poem combines ideas from two versions of the myth of Pandora's box, but it works in reverse. When Pandora opened her box, things flew out of it, or evaporated. Here, God's 'glass of blessings' bestows virtues on man, but reserves one, nameless, gift.

What do you think the gift is?

5   *span* – the span of a hand, with fingers extended.

14   *Nature* – this personification is an echo of the semi-divine status of nature in some classical, medieval and renaissance traditions.

Man, ere he is aware,
Hath put together a solemnity,
And drest his hearse, while he has breath
As yet to spare:
35 Yet Lord, instruct us so to die,
That all these dyings may be life in death.

The Pulley

When God at first made man,
Having a glass of blessings standing by;
Let us (said he) pour on him all we can:
Let the world's riches, which dispersèd lie,
5   Contract into a span.

So strength first made a way;
Then beauty flowed, then wisdom, honour, pleasure:
When almost all was out, God made a stay,
Perceiving that alone of all his treasure
10   Rest in the bottom lay.

For if I should (said he)
Bestow this jewel also on my creature,
He would adore my gifts instead of me,
And rest in Nature, not the God of Nature:
15   So both should losers be.

Yet let him keep the rest,
But keep them with repining restlessness:
Let him be rich and weary, that at least,
If goodness lead him not, yet weariness
20   May toss him to my breast.

Death

Herbert converts the frightful physical image of the skull into a positive, joyful companion.

> Note the image in line 11. How appropriate do you find it to the subject of the poem?

  1 *uncouth* – unknown.

 11 *fledge* – fully feathered, and therefore capable of flight.

 18 *Doomsday* – the final day, the Day of Judgement.

 24 *down* – feathers.

Death

Death, thou wast once an uncouth hideous thing,
                    Nothing but bones,
            The sad effect of sadder groans:
Thy mouth was open, but thou couldst not sing.

5   For we considered thee as at some six
                    Or ten years hence,
            After the loss of life and sense,
Flesh being turned to dust, and bones to sticks.

We lookt on this side of thee, shooting short;
10   Where we did find
            The shells of fledge souls left behind,
Dry dust, which sheds no tears, but may extort.

But since our Saviour's death did put some blood
                    Into thy face,
15   Thou art grown fair and full of grace,
Much in request, much sought for as a good.

For we do now behold thee gay and glad,
                    As at Doomsday;
            When souls shall wear their new array,
20 And all thy bones with beauty shall be clad.

Therefore we can go die as sleep, and trust
                    Half that we have
            Unto an honest faithful grave;
Making our pillows either down, or dust.

The final examples in this selection of Herbert's poetry are amongst his most personal poems: each seems to mark a stage in his private spiritual journey.

Redemption

This sonnet is allegorical, the parable of a relationship between landlord and tenant.

9 *straight* – at once, immediately.

10 *resorts* – places where people gather: here, the implication that they are of the upper classes, the fashionable world.

13–14 *Of thieves … died* – Matthew 9.10: 'And it came to pass, as Jesus sat at meat in the house, behold, many publicans and sinners came and sat down with him and his disciples.'

How does Herbert use paradox to provide meaning?

Affliction (I)

There are clearly autobiographical elements in this poem. It carries echoes of the plea contained in the Lord's Prayer: 'Lead us not into temptation …'.

How does the resolution contained in the final couplet affect your reading of this poem?

2 *brave* – splendid.

7 *furniture* – furnishings: the term as used here suggests the whole panoply of church regalia, including the vestments.

12 *mirth* – pleasure.

Redemption

Having been tenant long to a rich Lord,
    Not thriving, I resolvèd to be bold,
    And make a suit unto him, to afford
A new small-rented lease, and cancel th' old.
5   In heaven at his manor I him sought:
    They told me there, that he was lately gone
    About some land, which he had dearly bought
Long since on earth, to take possession.
I straight returned, and knowing his great birth,
10   Sought him accordingly in great resorts;
    In cities, theatres, gardens, parks, and courts:
At length I heard a ragged noise and mirth
    Of thieves and murderers: there I him espied,
    Who straight, *Your suit is granted*, said, and died.

Affliction (I)

When first thou didst entice to thee my heart,
             I thought the service brave:
So many joys I writ down for my part,
             Besides what I might have
5   Out of my stock of natural delights,
Augmented with thy gracious benefits.

I lookèd on thy furniture so fine,
             And made it fine to me:
Thy glorious household-stuff did me entwine,
10   And 'tice me unto thee.
Such stars I counted mine: both heav'n and earth
Paid me my wages in a world of mirth.

21 *strawed* – strewed, scattered.

24 *party* – a different side, i.e. in the contest between joy and grief.
25 *My flesh … pain* – my flesh began to complain in pain to my soul.
    cleave – cut into.

39–40 *Thou didst betray … gown* – God led him to study and preparation
       for the priesthood, rather than a secular career.

What pleasures could I want, whose King I served?
              Where joys my fellows were?
15   Thus argued into hopes, my thoughts reserved
              No place for grief or fear.
Therefore my sudden soul caught at the place,
And made her youth and fierceness seek thy face.

At first thou gav'st me milk and sweetnesses;
20   I had my wish and way:
My days were strawed with flow'rs and happiness;
              There was no month but May.
But with my years sorrow did twist and grow,
And made a party unawares for woe.

25   My flesh began unto my soul in pain,
              Sicknesses cleave my bones;
Consuming agues dwell in ev'ry vein,
              And tune my breath to groans.
Sorrow was all my soul; I scarce believed,
30   Till grief did tell me roundly, that I lived.

When I got health, thou took'st away my life,
              And more; for my friends die:
My mirth and edge was lost; a blunted knife
              Was of more use than I.
35   Thus thin and lean without a fence or friend,
I was blown through with ev'ry storm and wind.

Whereas my birth and spirit rather took
              The way that takes the town;
Thou didst betray me to a ling'ring book,
40   And wrap me in a gown.
I was entangled in the world of strife,
Before I had the power to change my life.

53   *cross-bias* – provide a counter-inclination: the metaphor is taken
     from the game of bowls.

60   *just* – having some purpose.

65–6   *though I am ... love thee not* – i.e. though I may have completely
       forgotten you, unless I love you, take from me the ability to do so.

Denial

How do form and meaning correspond in this poem?

Yet for I threatened oft the siege to raise,
                    Not simp'ring all mine age,
45 Thou often didst with academic praise
                    Melt and dissolve my rage.
I took thy sweetened pill, till I came where
I could not go away, nor persevere.

Yet lest perchance I should too happy be
50   In my unhappiness,
Turning my purge to food, thou throwest me
                    Into more sicknesses.
Thus doth thy power cross-bias me, not making
Thine own gift good, yet me from my ways taking.

55 Now I am here, that thou wilt do with me
                    None of my books will show:
I read, and sigh, and wish I were a tree;
                    For sure then I should grow
To fruit or shade: at least some bird would trust
60 Her household to me, and I should be just.

Yet, though thou troublest me, I must be meek;
                    In weakness must be stout.
Well, I will change the service, and go seek
                    Some other master out.
65 Ah my dear God! though I am clean forgot,
Let me not love thee, if I love thee not.

Denial

When my devotions could not pierce
                    Thy silent ears;
Then was my heart broken, as was my verse:
                    My breast was full of fears
5   And disorder:

10   *alarms* – summons to battle.

24   *nipt* – destroyed by frost.

The Collar

The title refers to the collar as an emblem of discipline, and is also a pun: 'choler' is anger.

In this poem, Herbert expresses frustration and fury with the discipline of God's service. How are you made aware of his emotions?

1   *board* – table, as in 'bed and board'. The implication here is of the communion table, or altar; the references to blood, wine and corn later in the poem reinforce this suggestion.

My bent thoughts, like a brittle bow,
Did fly asunder:
Each took his way; some would to pleasures go,
Some to the wars and thunder
10   Of alarms.

As good go any where, they say,
As to benumb
Both knees and heart, in crying night and day,
Come, come, my God, O come,
15   But no hearing.

O that thou shouldst give dust a tongue
To cry to thee,
And then not hear it crying! all day long
My heart was in my knee,
20   But no hearing.

Therefore my soul lay out of sight,
Untuned, unstrung:
My feeble spirit, unable to look right,
Like a nipt blossom, hung
25   Discontented.

O cheer and tune my heartless breast,
Defer no time;
That so thy favours granting my request,
They and my mind may chime,
30   And mend my rhyme.

The Collar

I struck the board, and cried, No more.
        I will abroad.
What? shall I ever sigh and pine?

5   *large as store* – as large as a store of goods, such as a warehouse.
6   *in suit* – asking favours.

9   *cordial* – restorative.

14 *bays* – laurels, from which, traditionally, triumphal wreaths were made.

26 *wink* – close the eyes.

29 *death's head* – a human skull was sometimes used as a focus for meditation, to remind its viewer of the brevity of human life and the inevitability of death.

My lines and life are free; free as the road,
5   Loose as the wind, as large as store.

                  Shall I be still in suit?
      Have I no harvest but a thorn
      To let me blood, and not restore
      What I have lost with cordial fruit?
10   Sure there was wine
      Before my sighs did dry it: there was corn
                  Before my tears did drown it.
      Is the year only lost to me?
                  Have I no bays to crown it?
15   No flowers, no garlands gay? all blasted?
                  All wasted?
      Not so, my heart: but there is fruit,
                  And thou hast hands.
      Recover all thy sigh-blown age
20   On double pleasures: leave thy cold dispute
      Of what is fit, and not. Forsake thy cage
                  Thy rope of sands,
      Which petty thoughts have made, and made to thee
      Good cable, to enforce and draw,
25   And be thy law,
      While thou didst wink and wouldst not see.
                  Away; take heed;
                  I will abroad.
      Call in thy death's head there: tie up thy fears.
30   He that forbears
                  To suit and serve his need,
                  Deserves his load.
      But as I raved and grew more fierce and wild
                  At every word,
35   Me thought I heard one calling, *Child!*
                  And I replied, *My Lord.*

Love (III)

'He that comes to the Sacrament hath the confidence of a guest, and he that kneels confesseth himself an unworthy one …' (*A Priest to the Temple: The Parson in Sacraments*)

This is the final poem in **The Temple**. Of the 'four last things' – Death, Judgement, Heaven and Hell – Herbert includes the first three, but substitutes 'Love' for 'Hell'.

> *From your reading of this selection of his poems, why do you think Herbert makes this substitution?*

12 *who made the eyes* – Psalm 94.9: 'he that formed the eye, shall he not see?'

16 *then I will serve* – as priest and as guest, sharing a meal in the true communion of friendship.

17 *taste my meat* – the 'meat' of the communion service is the blood and body of Christ: these three words are resonant with many biblical and liturgical echoes.

Love (III)

Love bade me welcome: yet my soul drew back,
    Guilty of dust and sin.
But quick-eyed Love, observing me grow slack
    From my first entrance in,
5 Drew nearer to me, sweetly questioning,
    If I lacked any thing.

A guest, I answered, worthy to be here:
    Love said, You shall be he.
I the'unkind, ungrateful? Ah my dear,
10   I cannot look on thee.
Love took my hand, and smiling did reply,
    Who made the eyes but I?

Truth Lord, but I have marred them: let my shame
    Go where it doth deserve.
15 And know you not, says Love, who bore the blame?
    My dear, then I will serve.
You must sit down, says Love, and taste my meat:
    So I did sit and eat.

FINIS

Glory be to God *on high*
    And on earth peace
      Good will towards men.

Thomas Carew (1594 – 1640)

Thomas Carew (pronounced Car*ey*) was born to a family of high social status; his father, Sir Matthew Carew, was a Master In Chancery and Doctor of Civil Law. Sir Matthew was already an elderly man when Thomas was born, and this fact, together with the financial problems which the family suffered, may have contributed to the eventual lack of understanding and sympathy between them.

Carew's education was conventional for someone of his time and class. He graduated from Merton College, Oxford, in 1612 and went on to study at the Middle Temple, as his father wished him to follow him into the legal profession. Carew, however, was not a diligent student, and soon moved on to gain employment as secretary to Sir Dudley Carleton, living with him during Sir Dudley's time as Ambassador at Venice, and later at The Hague. Some indiscreet writings, discovered by his employer, brought this period of Carew's life to a close. It had afforded him the opportunity to learn Italian, enabling him to read the poetry of Marino, whose lyrics Carew admired, and whom he may have met in Paris when he accompanied Sir Edward Herbert (brother of George Herbert) to Paris in 1619.

Carew's dismissal by Sir Dudley Carleton, and his apparent lack of any remorse, caused bad feeling between himself and his father, who died in 1618. Carew does not appear to have made much effort to live a diligent and sober life; he attached himself to court circles, and, while he was viewed with favour by King Charles I and many of the most influential in that circle, it was not until 1630 that he gained an official appointment, as a Gentleman of the Privy Chamber Extraordinary.

Carew's inclinations and talents drew him into the ranks of what was known as 'the tribe of Ben', friends and admirers of the poet and playwright Ben Jonson. Carew's poems circulated in manuscript amongst this group of talented and witty men. His own talents were recognized. He was referred to an 'excellent wit', and his poems were noted for their 'sharpness of the fancy and the elegancy of the language' (Clarendon). In 1634, he wrote a masque, *Coelum Britannicum*, which had settings by Inigo Jones, and which was performed before the king. Carew is likely to have heard John Donne preach, and his admiration for his work is aptly displayed in his *Elegy*, which was printed in an edition of Donne's poems in 1633.

Whilst gaining a sound reputation as a poet, Carew also led the pleasure-seeking life of a libertine. He appears to have taken little interest in political or religious matters, and only seems to have been concerned about the state of his soul when suffering from severe illness. However, while it is easy to be cynical about sickbed repentance, it must be remembered that Carew lived in an age when the concepts of sin and damnation were taken seriously. His flesh may have weakened in health, but the sincerity of some of his more serious poems does indicate a sense of self-condemnation:

> A pure flame may, shot by Almighty power
> Into my breast the earthy flame devour:
> My eyes, in penitential dew may steep
> That brine, which they for sensual love did weep:
>> from: *To my worthy friend Mr George Sandys*: 1638

Carew's intimations of mortality were justified, as he died in March 1639/40 after taking part in the King's expedition against Scotland. He appears to have been sincerely mourned, not least by the King, who 'always esteemed him to the last one of the most celebrated wits in his court'.

Carew's life and writings provide interesting contrasts with those of Crashaw, who, though he died nine years after Carew, was very much his contemporary. The choices of lifestyle made by both were very different, and this is reflected in their poetry, while they shared to some degree the cultural influence of Italian writers. Carew, the courtier and wit, was very much a 'Cavalier' poet, and it should be remembered that his early death removed him from the experience of the English Civil War, which was a sobering and influential episode in both political and artistic life for many of those who lived through it. The examples of Carew's work printed here include the *Elegy* for John Donne, which is evidence of the debt which Carew felt he owed, and a sincere encomium from one craftsman-poet to another. The rest of the selection provides examples of Carew's love poetry, illustrating the careful craftsmanship, as well as the energy and wit, of his writing. Control of form and clarity of expression owe much to Jonson, whilst the lyrical qualities of these poems may reflect the influence of Italian poetry.

An Elegy upon the Death of the Dean of Paul's, Dr John Donne

This poem, written as a tribute to the poet and divine, takes the form of an elegy. This poetic term has been applied to various kinds of poetry at different periods, From the 16th century, it was usually applied to reflective poetry. Many of Donne's longer early poems bear that label, though in his case many of them seem to be more a celebration of sexual conquests, in which the reflective element is the least noticeable! Later, the term became associated with mourning, Carew's poem seems to cover both definitions: he mourns Donne's death whilst reflecting on his poetic achievement. The poem was published with an edition of Donne's own poetry in 1633.

Consider why Carew uses so many classical references. What does he most admire about Donne as a poet?

4   *dough-baked* – imperfectly baked, implying flat, tasteless.

5   *unscissored* – with uncut hair, a sign of mourning.

6   *rhetoric* – Greek in origin, this was the art of persuasive speaking. Literary rhetoric was concerned with the organization and embellishment of writing, and was part of education up to the seventeenth century.

7   *the sand that measures it* – the reference is to an hour-glass, which measures time by the passage of sand from an upper to a lower glass chamber (like an egg-timer).

17   *rapes* – used in the sense of seizure, without its modern, almost exclusively sexual, connotation. However, the word does have a resonance that may remind the reader of the language of Donne's *Holy Sonnet* beginning 'Batter my heart, three-person'd God', in which the imagery appears to subsume the spiritual within the physical.

22   *Delphic* – the sanctuary of Apollo, god of music and poetry, is at Delphi, in Greece.

23   *Promethean* – in the Greek myth, Prometheus brought fire from heaven to give to mankind.

25   *pedantic* – a pendant is one who insists on strict and slavish adherence to formal rules. Carew suggests that Donne's poetry revived the art which had been choked by sterile techniques.

30   *Licentious* – used in its early meaning of 'unrestrained'.

31   *mimic* – imitative.

An Elegy upon the Death of the Dean of Paul's, Dr John Donne

    Can we not force from widowed poetry,
    Now thou art dead (great Donne) one elegy
    To crown thy hearse? Why yet did we not trust,
    Though with unkneaded, dough-baked prose, thy dust,
5   Such as the unscissored churchman from the flower
    Of fading rhet'ric, short-lived as his hour,
    Dry as the sand that measures it, should lay
    Upon the ashes, on the funeral day?
    Have we no voice, nor tune? Didst thou dispense
10 Through all our language, both the words and sense?
    'Tis a sad truth; the pulpit may her plain
    And sober Christian precepts still retain;
    Doctrines it may, and wholesome uses, frame,
    Grave homilies and lectures. But the flame
15 Of thy brave soul (that shot such heat and light,
    As burnt our earth, and made our darkness bright,
    Committed holy rapes upon our will,
    Did through the eye the melting heart distil,
    And the deep knowledge of dark truths so teach
20 As sense might judge, what fancy could not reach;)
    Must be desired for ever. So the fire
    That fills with spirit and heat the Delphic choir,
    Which, kindled first by thy Promethean breath,
    Glowed here a while, lies quenched now in thy death.
25 The Muses' garden with pedantic weeds
    O'erspread, was purged by thee; the lazy seeds
    Of servile imitation thrown away,
    And fresh invention planted; thou didst pay
    The debts of our penurious bankrupt age;
30 Licentious thefts, that make poetic rage
    A mimic fury, when our souls must be

32   *Anacreon* – Anacreon was a sixth-century BC Greek lyric poet. Though only a very few of his poems survive, a large collection of 'anacreontic' poems of unknown origin was printed in Paris in 1554, and many seventeenth-century poets imitated these in their writing.

32–3   *or … or* – this doubled conjunction introducing alternatives was common in the seventeenth century. We would say 'either … or'. The idea pursued in these lines is that Carew's contemporaries can only imitate earlier writers, and have no real poetic passion of their own.

33   *Pindar* – Another early Greek lyric poet, whose odes were widely admired and imitated by seventeenth-century (and later) poets.

40   *Orpheus* – the legendary Greek hero, who was the son of Apollo and the muse Calliope: he was renowned as a musician.
       ancient brood – early (classical) poets.

43   *exchequer* – treasury. Carew suggests that even the classical and mythic poets would have drawn inspiration from Donne's poetry.

50(ff.)   *our stubborn language bends* – the idea is the Donne's masterful handling of the English language (which may be regarded as less musical than the classical and romance languages) empowered him to produce ideas and images which had a strength and force lacking in works written in more mellifluous languages.

51   *tough thick-rib'd hoops* – the conceit is based on the iron hoops which bind together the wooden staves of a barrel.

56   *rifled* – robbed, pillaged.

62   *libertines* – implying dissolute, frivolous.

64   *of gods and goddesses* – the subject-matter of slighter poets, prior to Donne.

66   *Metamorphoses* – Ovid's **Metamorphoses** were stories of gods and goddesses and provided much poetic material.

69   *ballad* - simple, popular verses or songs.

Possessed, or with Anacreon's ecstasy,
Or Pindar's, not their own; the subtle cheat
Of sly exchanges, and the juggling feat
35 Of two-edged words, or whatsoever wrong
By ours was done the Greek, or Latin tongue,
Thou hast redeemed, and opened us a mine
Of rich and pregnant fancy; drawn a line
Of masculine expression, which had good
40 Old Orpheus seen, or all the ancient brood
Our superstitious fools admire and hold
Their lead more precious than thy burnished gold,
Thou hadst been their exchequer, and no more
They each in other's dust, had raked for ore.
45 Thou shalt yield no precedence, but of time,
And the blind fate of language, whose tuned chime
More charms the outward sense; yet thou mayst claim
From so great disadvantage greater fame,
Since to the awe of thy imperious wit
50 Our stubborn language bends, made only fit
With her tough thick-rib'd hoops to gird about
Thy giant fancy, which had proved too stout
For their soft melting phrases. As in time
They had the start, so did they cull the prime
55 Buds of invention many a hundred year,
And left the rifled fields, besides the fear
To touch their harvest; yet from those bare lands
Of what is purely thine, thy only hands,
(And that their smallest work) have gleanèd more
60 Than all those times and tongues could reap before.
    But thou art gone, and thy strict laws will be
Too hard for libertines in poetry.
They will recall the goodly exiled train
Of gods and goddesses, which in thy just reign
65 Were banished nobler poems; now with these,
The silenced tales o'th' *Metamorphoses*,
Shall stuff their lines, and swell the windy page,
Till verse, refined by thee, in this last age,
Turn ballad rhyme, or those old idols be

70   *apostasy* – renunciation of faith.

77–8   *numbers … accents* – technical poetic terms.

84   *bays* – in classical times, the winner of a poetic contest was awarded a crown of bay leaves.

97   *flamen* – a priest who serves a particular god.

98   *Apollo's . . God's* – Carew refers to the two dominant inspirations for Donne's poetry, the mythic, pagan god of poetry, and the Christian God.

70   Adored again with new apostasy.
       O, pardon me, that break with untuned verse
The reverend silence that attends thy hearse,
Whose awful solemn murmurs were to thee,
More than these faint lines, a loud elegy,
75   That did proclaim in a dumb eloquence
The death of all the arts, whose influence,
Grown feeble, in these panting numbers lies
Gasping short-winded accents, and so dies:
So doth the swiftly turning wheel not stand
80   In the instant we withdraw the moving hand,
But some small time retain a faint weak course
By virtue of the first impulsive force:
And so, whilst I cast on thy funeral pile
The crown of bays, oh, let it crack awhile,
85   And spit disdain, till the devouring flashes
Suck all the moisture up, then turn to ashes.
       I will not draw the envy to engross
All thy perfections, or weep all the loss;
Those are too numerous for an elegy,
90   And this too great to be expressed by me.
Though every pen should share a distinct part,
Yet art thou theme enough to tire all art;
Let others carve the rest, it shall suffice
I on thy tomb this epitaph incise.

95   *Here lies a king, that ruled as he thought fit*
      The universal monarchy of wit;
      Here lie two flamens, and both those, the best,
      Apollo's first, at last, the true God's priest.

Mediocrity in Love Rejected

2 *torrid, or frozen zone* – the reference is to a geographical definition of the divisions of the earth into five zones, bounded by circles which are parallel to the equator. The torrid zone is the central belt between the tropics of Cancer and Capricorn, and therefore hottest. The frozen zone is the polar regions.

8 *Danaë* – The daughter of the King of Argos who, according to the myth, was visited by Zeus in the form of a shower of gold. She was cast adrift on the sea by her father, together with her son Perseus, but subsequently rescued. The story makes the opening of 1.9 particularly apt.

11 *vulture-hopes* – an allusion to the vulture which perpetually tears at the liver of Prometheus, as a punishment for giving fire to mankind. Carew suggests that he is devoured by hope.

To My Inconstant Mistress

1 *excommunicate* – literally, one who is cast out of the body of the Church. This concept would have had real force in Carew's time.

15 *apostasy* – rejection of faith. The use of the language of religion to carry a conceit is typical of much metaphysical poetry.

Mediocrity in Love Rejected

Give me more love, or more disdain;
    The torrid, or the frozen zone
Bring equal ease unto my pain;
    The temperate affords me none:
5 Either extreme, of love or hate,
Is sweeter than a calm estate.

Give me a storm; if it be love,
    Like Danaë in that golden shower,
I swim in pleasure; if it prove
10   Disdain, that torrent will devour
My vulture-hopes; and he's possessed
Of heaven, that's but from hell released:
    Then crown my joys, or cure my pain;
    Give me more love, or more disdain.

To My Inconstant Mistress

When thou, poor excommunicate
    From all the joys of love, shalt see
The full reward, and glorious fate
    Which my strong faith shall purchase me,
5   Then curse thine own inconstancy.

A fairer hand than thine shall cure
    That heart, which thy false oaths did wound;
And to my soul, a soul more pure
    Than thine, shall by love's hand be bound,
10   And both with equal glory crowned.

Then shalt thou weep, entreat, complain
    To love, as I did once to thee;
When all thy tears shall be as vain
    As mine were then, for thou shalt be
15   Damned for thy false apostasy.

5   *Celia* – a fictitious name for the subject of the poem: it is very
    unlikely that it was addressed to a specifically-named woman. The
    use of such a name harks back to the poetry of Catullus, a Roman
    poet whose work was much admired by the 'tribe of Ben' to which
    Carew belonged. Catullus's line 'Vivamus, mea Lesbia, atque
    amemus' (Let us live, my Lesbia, and let us love) was echoed by
    Jonson in his play *Volpone*: 'Come, my Celia, let us prove/While we
    may, the sports of love.' Carew also uses the name in other poems.

7   *golden fleece* – her golden hair. The echo of a classical allusion
    underlines the image of timelessness.

Boldness in Love

2   *marigold* – the marigold was so called in honour of the Virgin Mary.
    'Virgin leaves' in l.8 echoes this allusion.

5   *planet of the day* – the sun.

9   *fond boy* – 'fond' is used in its earlier meaning of 'foolish'. As in other
    poems, the addressee of the poem is likely to be fictitious.

15 *Celia* – see above.

Persuasions to enjoy

If the quick spirits in your eye
Now languish, and anon must dye;
If every sweet, and every grace,
Must fly from that forsaken face:
5   Then (Celia) let us reap our joys,
    E'er time such goodly fruit destroys.

Or, if that golden fleece must grow
For ever, free from aged snow;
If those bright suns must know no shade,
10 Nor your fresh beauties ever fade:
The fear not (Celia) to bestow,
What still being gathered, still must grow,
    Thus, either Time his sickle brings
    In vain, or else in vain his wings.

Boldness in Love

Mark how the bashful morn, in vain
Courts the amorous marigold,
With sighing blasts, and weeping rain;
Yet she refuses to unfold.
5 But when the planet of the day
Approacheth with his powerful ray,
Then she spreads, then she receives
His warmer beams into her virgin leaves.
So shalt thou thrive in love, fond boy;
10 If thy tears and sighs discover
Thy grief, thou never shalt enjoy
The just reward of a bold lover;
But when with moving accents thou
Shalt constant faith and service vow,
15 Thy Celia shall receive those charms
With open ears, and with unfolded arms.

A Song

1   *Jove* – another name for Jupiter (or Zeus).

3–4   *For in ... sleep* – a complex conceit, which can be interpreted as suggesting that the primal cause, or origin, of the roses, can be found in the depths and dawning of her beauty.
A reading of the poem can be based on an extension of this idea, relating the beauty of the woman to the finest things in nature.

6   *golden atoms* – sunbeams.

11   *dividing* – warbling, or descanting, as in singing.

16   *sphere* – the concept of the fixed stars, in the stellatum. beyond the sphere of Saturn, which was long thought to be the furthest planet from Earth. The conceit draws on medieval cosmology, which saw the universe as a series of spheres, with Heaven beyond them,

18   *phoenix* – see page 114.

A Song

Ask me no more where Jove bestows,
When June is past, the fading rose:
For in your beauty's orient deep
These flowers as in their causes, sleep.

5 Ask me no more whither doth stray
The golden atoms of the day:
For in pure love heaven did prepare
Those powders to enrich your hair.

Ask me no more whither doth haste
10 The nightingale, when May is past:
For in your sweet dividing throat
She winters and keeps warm her note.

Ask me no more where those stars light,
That downwards fall in dead of night:
15 For in your eyes they sit, and there,
Fixèd become, as in their sphere.

Ask me no more if east or west,
The phoenix builds her spicy nest:
For unto you at last she flies,
20 And in your fragrant bosom dies.

Richard Crashaw (1612/13 – 1649)

Richard Crashaw was the son of a well-known Puritan theological scholar, who was a preacher at the Temple, in London. Both his mother and his stepmother died before Crashaw was nine, and his father died in 1626. About three years later Crashaw was sent to be educated at Charterhouse, and then to Pembroke College, Cambridge.

It was at Pembroke that Crashaw experienced a fundamentally different religious ethos from the austere culture of the Puritans. Pembroke was dominated by High Anglican churchmen. Here, he became friendly with Nicholas Ferrar, who was a close friend of George Herbert, and who was entrusted with the manuscript of Herbert's poems, *The Temple*. Ferrar and other members of his family established an Anglican religious community on their estate at Little Gidding, founded on principles of private devotion and study combined with public charity. Crashaw visited Little Gidding frequently, perhaps using it as a retreat.

In 1635, Crashaw became a Fellow of Peterhouse, which was the centre in Cambridge of High Churchmanship. Whether or not Crashaw took Holy Orders is uncertain, but he did hold an office of some kind at Little St Mary's. This was a quiet and retired life, during which Crashaw was able to indulge his interest and talents in drawing and music, as well as learning Spanish and Italian, which was to be of great benefit in his later life. The reading and translation which he undertook during this time influenced both his art as a poet and his religious beliefs. The sensuous, extravagant style of the Italian poet Marino, as well as the writings of Spanish mystics, provided some of the inspiration for the baroque imagery and intense re-creation of highly-charged religious experience which are the hallmark of Crashaw's religious poetry.

The tensions between plainness and ornament, Puritan and High Church, which Crashaw's personal life seems to reflect, came to a kind of climax for him some time between 1643 and 1645. In 1643, Peterhouse and Little St Mary's both became the victims of the Parliamentary purge of religious images, which stripped chapels and churches of pictures, stained glass windows and statues. Crashaw left Cambridge, probably for Leyden, and after a while (during which he may have returned briefly to England) he became a convert to the Roman Catholic church and fled to Paris.

Queen Henrietta Maria, wife of Charles I (who was then embroiled in the English Civil War), had a court in exile in Paris. The poet Abraham Cowley, a Cambridge friend of Crashaw's, used his influence to interest the Queen in Crashaw, and she provided him with letters of introduction to clerics in Rome. Thus he gained employment, principally with Cardinal Palotta.

Despite the extravagance of his verse, Crashaw was, in his private life, an austere man, perhaps as a result of the earliest influence in his life, the Puritan household in London. He was not at home in the Byzantine complexities which dominated the households of the Princes of the Church of Rome, nor was he comfortable with the low standard of morals which existed within their retinues. Palotta eventually appointed him to a minor post at the Santa Casa of Loreto, the shrine which contains what was believed to be the house of the Virgin Mary, said to have been transported by angels from Palestine. Devoted to the Virgin Mary and naturally reclusive, Crashaw could have been happy there, but it was a brief refuge. Less than six months after taking up the appointment, he died, in the August of 1649.

Crashaw is principally remembered for his religious poetry. A collection entitled *Steps to the Temple* was published in 1646, to which was appended a section of secular poems, the *Delights of the Muses*. A posthumous collection was published in 1652, under the title *Carmen Deo Nostro* (A Song to our God).

His wide-ranging artistic interests, encompassing music and the plastic arts as well as poetry, were part of the formative influence on Crashaw the poet. He could produce a singing lyrical line and images which are both rich and rapturous. But the line can be over-cloyed with sweetness at times, and, at its worst, the imagery verges on the ridiculous. Crashaw's work needs to be viewed, however, in the context of the high baroque, whose visual images dominated the artistic expression and architecture of Roman Catholicism during the middle years of the seventeenth century. The *Hymn to Saint Theresa* is the poetic equivalent of the Bernini statue of that saint in St Peter's, Rome, and the mystic ecstasies which Crashaw celebrates are those to be found in the paintings of Murillo and El Greco.

Crashaw's writing is represented here by just two long poems. They are characteristic of his most mature writing, combining mysticism and celebration, and arising from the faith which became central to his life and work.

A Hymn of the Nativity, sung as by the Shepherds

The form of the poem is choric, with two main speaking voices, introduced by a chorus which echoes their words throughout, and speaks the final extended chorus. This form has some of its closest origins in the masque, elaborately staged musical entertainments popular at Court. Here, Crashaw gives the two main speakers invented names of classical origin.

How appropriate is the word 'hymn' in the title of the poem?

A Hymn of the Nativity, sung as by the Shepherds

Come, we shepherds whose blest sight
Hath met love's noon in nature's night;
Come, lift we up our loftier song
And wake the sun that lies too long.

5 To all our world of well-stol'n joy
   He slept, and dreamed of no such thing;
While we found out Heav'n's fairer eye,
   And kissed the cradle of our King.
Tell him he rises now too late,
10 To show us aught worth looking at.

Tell him we now can show him more
   Than he e'er showed to mortal sight,
Than he himself e'er saw before,
   Which to be seen needs not his light.
15 Tell him, Tityrus, where th'hast been;
Tell him, Thyrsis, what th'hast seen.

Tityrus

Gloomy night embraced the place
   Where the noble Infant lay;
The Babe looked up and showed his face:
20   In spite of darkness, it was day:
It was thy day, Sweet! and did rise
Not from the east, but from thine eyes.

Chorus. It was thy day, Sweet, [etc.]

31 *balmy nest* – balm is an aromatic oil, used for anointing, soothing or
    healing. 'Balm of Gilead' is a fragrant resin used as an ointment.
    Here, the image seems to combine the ideas of kingship (a ruler is
    anointed with holy oil at the time of coronation) and Christ as
    healer of mankind's ills.

42 *huge* – used here in the sense of 'significant' or 'very great', not
    referring to size. 'Mighty' (l.45) has much the same meaning,
    referring to status.

46 *phoenix* – the bird of fire, a symbol of the Resurrection. It is reborn
    from the fire in which it consumes itself. It appears in many
    mythologies. One Christian myth states that it did not share the sin
    of Eve as it did not eat the forbidden fruit in the Garden of Eden.

Winter chid aloud, and sent
25   The angry north to wage his wars.
The north forgot his fierce intent,
    And left perfumes instead of scars.
By those sweet eyes' persuasive pow'rs,
Where he meant frost, he scattered flowers.

30   *Chorus.* By those sweet eyes' [etc.]

    Both

We saw thee in thy balmy nest,
    Young dawn of our eternal day!
We saw thine eyes break from their east,
    And chase the trembling shades away.
35   We saw thee, and we blessed the sight,
We saw thee by thine own sweet light.

    Tityrus

Poor world (said I) what wilt thou do
    To entertain this starry stranger?
Is this the best thou canst bestow,
40   A cold and not too cleanly manager?
Contend, ye powers of heav'n and earth,
To fit a bed for this huge birth.

    Chorus. Contend, ye powers [etc.]

    Thyrsis

Proud world (said I) cease your contest,
45   And let the mighty babe alone.
The phoenix builds the phoenix' nest
    Love's architecture is his own.

48 *embraves* – this seems to be an invented word, on the same lines as 'empower'.

51 *curl'd drops* – snow.

58 *obsequious seraphims* – 'obsequious' here means obedient, attentive. The modern idea of 'servile' is not appropriate. Seraphims were members of the first order of the hierarchy of angels. This concept was popularised in the fifth century, and remained as part of accepted scholarship for many centuries, though by Crashaw's time it is likely to have been regarded as archaic, therefore, probably, appropriate for the style of this poem. The orders were (1) Seraphim, Cherubim and Thrones, (2) Dominions, Virtues and Powers, (3) Principalities, Archangels and Angels.

63 *Your down so warm, will pass for pure?* – compare this with the same concept used by Donne in *Air and Angels*. Angels were pure spirit, and in order to take on a body they had to clothe themselves in air, an element less pure than themselves.

The Babe whose birth embraves this morn
Made his own bed ere he was born.

50   *Chorus.* The Babe whose birth [etc.]

Tityrus

I saw the curl'd drops, soft and slow,
      Come hovering o'er the place's head,
Off'ring their whitest sheets of snow,
      To furnish the fair Infant's bed.
55 Forbear, (said I) be not too bold;
Your fleece is white, but 'tis too cold.

Chorus. Forbear said I, [etc.]

Thyrsis

I saw the obsequious seraphims
      Their rosy fleece of fire bestow
60 For well they now can spare their wings,
      Since Heav'n itself lies here below.
Well done (said I) but are you sure
Your down so warm will pass for pure?

Chorus. Well done said I, [etc.]

Tityrus

65 No, no, your king's not yet to seek
      Where to repose his royal head,
See, see, how soon his new-bloomed cheek
      'Twixt mother's breasts is gone to bed.
Sweet choice (said I) no way but so,
70 Not to lie cold, yet sleep in snow.

Chorus. Sweet choice said I, [etc.]

88   *rarely temper'd* – the image draws on the idea of tempering metal, with 'rarely' meaning 'finely'. Metal is tempered, or strengthened, by the application of heat (fire) and cold (water).

95–6   *mother-diamonds tries/The points of her young Eagle's eyes* – this is a complex conceit. It is probably best to respond to what seem to be the underlying ideas, rather than try to work out exact analogies, or to interpret the lines. Mother-diamonds may refer to tears, but it is the child who is weeping. The Eagle is the king of birds, therefore a fitting image for the Christ-child. In hunting, a point is a spot at which a straight run is made. There is a combination of gentleness and strength, female and male, richness and ferocity, in these two lines.

97   *flies* – a derogatory term sometimes used for courtiers, usually of the parasitic kind. In Act V scene ii of *Hamlet*, Hamlet refers to the courtier Osric as a 'waterfly'.

We saw thee in thy balmy nest,
   Bright dawn of our eternal day,
We saw thine eyes break from their east
75   And chase the trembling shades away.
We saw thee, and we blessed the sight;
We saw thee, by thine own sweet light.

     Chorus. We saw thee, [etc.]

  Full Chorus

Welcome, all wonders in one sight!
80   Eternity shut in a span,
Summer in winter, day in night,
   Heaven in earth, and God in man.
Great little one! whose all-embracing birth
Lifts earth to heav'n, stoops heav'n to earth.

85 Welcome, though nor to gold nor silk,
   To more than Caesar's birthright is;
Two sister-seas of virgin-milk,
   With many a rarely tempered kiss,
That breathes at once both maid and mother,
90 Warms in the one, cools in the other.

She sings thy tears asleep, and dips
   Her kisses in thy weeping eye,
She spreads the red leaves of thy lips,
   That in their buds yet blushing lie.
95 She 'gainst those mother-diamonds tries
   The points of her young Eagle's eyes.

Welcome, though not to those gay flies
   Gilded i'th'beams of earthly kings,
Slippery souls in smiling eyes,

104   *Maia* – May.

107   *dread* – 'revered' or 'honoured', rather than 'feared'.

113–14   *Till burnt ... sacrifice* – the concept of the pagan burnt offering to
the gods is combined with the idea of purification through
redemption, which Christ's birth, and death, made possible for
humanity.

Hymn to Saint Teresa

Saint Teresa of Avila lived between 1515 and 1582. She founded a reformed
order of Carmelite nuns. Well-known for her mysticism, she wrote an
autobiography which was published in English in 1642. Crashaw drew on this
for his poem, focusing especially on her attempt, as a child, to court
martyrdom by preaching to the Moors, and her mystic vision of a flesh-
piercing fiery dart.

*Note the effect of Crashaw's combination of images of childish innocence and
death, joy and pain.*

7   *lusty* – strong, vigorous.

100 But to poor shepherds, homespun things,
  Whose wealth's their flock, whose wit, to be
   Well read in their simplicity.

  Yet when young April's husband-showers
   Shall bless the fruitful Maia's bed,
105 We'll bring the first-born of her flowers
   To kiss thy feet and crown thy head.
  To thee, dread Lamb! whose love must keep
   The shepherds more than they the sheep;

  To thee, meek Majesty! soft King
110 Of simple graces and sweet loves,
  Each of us his lamb will bring,
   Each his pair of silver doves;
  Till burnt at last in fire of thy fair eyes,
   Ourselves become our own best sacrifice.

Hymn to Saint Teresa

Lord, thou art absolute sole Lord
Of life and death. To prove the word,
We'll now appeal to none of all
Those thy old soldiers, great and tall
5 Ripe men of martyrdom, that could reach down
With strong arms their triumphant crown:
Such as could with lusty breath
Speak loud into the face of death
Their great Lord's glorious name; to none
10 Of those whose spacious bosoms spread a throne
For love at large to fill. Spare blood and sweat,
And see him take a private seat,
Making his mansion in the mild
And milky soul of a soft child.

32 *nonage* – immaturity.

47 *Moors* – North Africans and Muslims, who occupied an extensive part of Spain for many years.

15 Scarce has she learnt to lisp the name
      Of martyr, yet she thinks it shame
      Life should so long play with that breath
      Which spent can buy so brave a death.
      She never undertook to know
20 What death with love should have to do;
      Nor has she e'er yet understood
      Why to show love she should shed blood;
      Yet though she cannot tell you why,
      She can love and she can die.
25   Scarce has she blood enough to make
      A guilty sword blush for her sake;
      Yet has she a heart dares hope to prove
      How much less strong is death than love.
          Be love but there, let poor six years
30 Be posed with the maturest fears
      Man trembles at, you straight shall find
      Love knows no nonage, nor the mind.
      'Tis love, not years or limbs, that can
      Make the martyr or the man.
35   Love touched her heart, and lo it beats
      High, and burns with such brave heats,
      Such thirsts to die, as dares drink up
      A thousand cold deaths in one cup.
      Good reason; for she breathes all fire.
40 Her weak breast heaves with strong desire
      Of what she may with fruitless wishes
      Seek for amongst her mother's kisses.
          Since 'tis not to be had at home,
      She'll travel for a martyrdom.
45 No home for hers confesses she
      But where she may a martyr be.
          She'll to the Moors, and trade with them
      For this unvalued diadem.
      She'll offer them her dearest breath,
50 With Christ's name in 't, in change for death.
      She'll bargain with them, and will give
      Them God, and teach them how to live

65 *Spouse* – partner in marriage. As a nun, Teresa was a 'bride of Christ'.

71 *race* – an archaic meaning of this word is to scratch or to mark with a line. Used in this context, this meaning may be intended. Alternatively, Crashaw may have had in mind the word 'raze', meaning 'to destroy'.

In him; or if they this deny,
For him she'll teach them how to die.
55 So shall she leave amongst them sown
Her Lord's blood, or at least her own.
  Farewell then, all the world! adieu,
Teresa is no more for you.
Farewell, all pleasures, sports and joys,
60 (Never till now esteemèd toys)
Farewell, whatever dear may be,
Mother's arms, or father's knee;
Farewell house, and farewell home!
She's for the Moors and martyrdom.
65 Sweet, not so fast! lo, thy fair Spouse
Whom thou seek'st with so swift vows
Calls thee back, and bids thee come,
T' embrace a milder martyrdom.
  Blest powers forbid thy tender life
70 Should bleed upon a barbarous knife;
Or some base hand have power to race
Thy breast's chaste cabinet, and uncase
A soul kept there so sweet. Oh no;
Wise Heav'n will never have it so:
75 Thou art Love's victim, and must die
A death more mystical and high,
Into Love's arms thou shalt let fall
A still surviving funeral.
  His is the dart must make the death
80 Whose stroke shall taste thy hallowed breath;
A dart thrice dipped in that rich flame,
Which writes thy spouse's radiant name
Upon the roof of Heav'n, where aye
It shines, and with a sovereign ray
85 Beats bright upon the burning faces
Of souls which in that name's sweet graces
Find everlasting smiles; so rare,
So spiritual, pure, and fair
Must be th'immortal instrument,
90 Upon whose choice point shall be sent,

94   *seraphims* – see page 116.

109   *balsam* – aromatic resin, used as base for fragrances and medicinal
      ointments.

123–4 *The moon of maiden stars, thy white/Mistress* – the Virgin Mary.

A life so loved; and that there be
Fit executioners for thee,
The fair'st and first-born sons of fire,
Blest seraphims, shall leave their choir
95 And turn Love's soldiers, upon thee
To exercise their archery.
    Oh how oft shalt thou complain
Of a sweet and subtle pain!
Of intolerable joys!
100 Of a death, in which who dies
Loves his death, and dies again,
And would for ever so be slain!
And lives and dies, and knows not why
To live; but that he thus may never leave to die!
105   How kindly will thy gentle heart
Kiss the sweetly killing dart!
And close in his embraces keep
Those delicious wounds, that weep
Balsam to heal themselves with. Thus
110 When these thy deaths, so numerous,
Shall all at last die into one,
And melt thy soul's sweet mansion;
Like a soft lump of incense, hasted
By too hot a fire, and wasted
115 Into perfuming clouds, so fast
Shalt thou exhale to Heav'n at last
In a resolving sigh, and then,
Oh what?. . ask not the tongues of men
Angels cannot tell. Suffice,
120 Thyself shall feel thine own full joys
And hold them fast for ever. There,
So soon as thou shalt first appear,
The moon of maiden stars, thy white
Mistress, attended by such bright
125 Souls as thy shining self, shall come
And in her first ranks make thee room;
Where 'mongst her snowy family
Immortal welcomes wait for thee.

142 *constellation* – a group of stars.

154 *account* – a record.

Oh, what delight, when reveal'd life shall stand
130 And teach thy lips Heav'n with his hand,
On which thou now mayst to thy wishes
Heap up thy consecrated kisses.
What joys shall seize thy soul when she,
Bending her blessed eyes on thee,
135 (Those second smiles of Heav'n) shall dart
Her mild rays through thy melting heart!
    Angels, thy old friends, there shall greet thee,
Glad at their own home now to meet thee.
All thy good works which went before
140 And waited for thee, at the door,
Shall own thee there; and all in one
Weave a constellation
Of crowns, with which the King, thy spouse,
Shall build up thy triumphant brows.
145 All thy old woes shall now smile on thee,
And thy pains sit bright upon thee;
All thy sorrows here shall shine,
All thy sufferings be divine.
Tears shall take comfort and turn gems,
150 And wrongs repent to diadems.
Even thy deaths shall live, and new
Dress the soul that erst they slew
Thy wounds shall blush to such bright scars
As keep account of the Lamb's wars.
155 Those rare works where thou shalt leave writ
Love's noble history, with wit
Taught thee by none but him, while here
They feed our souls, shall clothe thine there.
Each heav'nly word by whose hid flame
160 Our hard hearts shall strike fire, the same
Shall flourish on thy brows, and be
Both fire to us, and flame to thee,
Whose light shall live bright in thy face
By glory, in our hearts by grace.
165 Thou shalt look round about and see
Thousands of crowned souls throng to be

172 *zone* – girdle.

Themselves thy crown; sons of thy vows,
The virgin-births with which thy sovereign Spouse
Made fruitful thy fair soul. Go now
170 And with them all about thee bow
To him. Put on (he'll say) put on
(My rosy love) that thy rich zone
Sparkling with the sacred flames
Of thousand souls, whose happy names
175 Heav'n keeps upon thy score. (Thy bright
Life brought them first to kiss the light
That kindled them to stars). And so
Thou with the Lamb, thy Lord, shalt go,
And whereso'er he sets his white
180 Steps, walk with him those ways of light
Which who in death would live to see
Must learn in life to die like thee.

Andrew Marvell (1621 – 1678)

Andrew Marvell was born in Yorkshire and was educated at Hull Grammar School and Trinity College, Cambridge. He went to London after graduating from Cambridge in 1639, and spent four years travelling in Europe, possibly as a tutor, possibly as a government agent; during this time he learned Spanish, Italian, French and Dutch.

In 1650, the year after the execution of Charles I and the year of Cromwell's Irish and Scottish campaigns, he became tutor to Mary, the daughter of the Parliamentarian Lord Fairfax, at Appleton House, in Yorkshire, a place which inspired many of his lyric poems, including *The Garden* and *Upon Appleton House*. He spent two years there, and came to admire his employer; Fairfax's moral principles had led him to retire from public life. Then, in 1653, Marvell was appointed tutor to William Dutton, a ward of Oliver Cromwell.

Although during his early life Marvell's inclinations and connections seem to have been mainly Royalist, he was now firmly linked to the Parliamentarian party. He wrote songs for the marriage of Cromwell's daughter Mary, and in 1657 was appointed Latin secretary to the Council of State, a position for which the poet John Milton had recommended him four years earlier. Later, Marvell was to repay this debt to Milton by defending him against persecution after the Restoration in 1660. Marvell took part in the funeral procession of Oliver Cromwell in 1658, together with his fellow poets Dryden and Milton, and pledged allegiance to Cromwell's son Richard in a poem on the Protector's death.

In 1659 Marvell was elected as one of the two MPs for Hull, and continued to represent that constituency after the Restoration. The diarist John Aubrey wrote of him: 'His native town of Hull loved him so well that they elected him for their representative in parliament, and gave him an honourable pension to maintain him.'

In the early 1660s Marvell travelled widely on embassies, accompanying the Earl of Carlisle to Russia, Sweden and Denmark, but he maintained his opposition to the elements of the establishment which he saw as anti-libertarian and dangerous to the English people, publishing many satires and political pamphlets. He died in 1678.

Andrew Marvell's life spanned one of the most turbulent periods in English history, and his career, experiences and writings reflect this. The tensions produced by the opposition of the Stuart monarchy, in the person of Charles I, and the Commonwealth, to an extent personified by the Protector, Oliver Cromwell, are the background against which the writings of all those who were active in literature at that time must be seen. Marvell, in his life and in his writings, seems to exemplify this. As a young man at Cambridge, he wrote a Latin and Greek poem congratulating Charles I on the birth of a daughter, and seems to have flirted briefly with the Jesuits, before being reclaimed by his father, a parson of Calvinist leanings. Other early poems underline Royalist connections, including his elegy for Lord Francis Villiers, killed in the Civil War in 1648.

Later, Marvell's career linked him closely to the Parliamentarian camp, and, after the Restoration, he was renowned for his satirical writings, which opposed corruption and religious bigotry; these writings were admired and read widely, even by Charles II. Trusted to travel on diplomatic missions, Marvell was also under surveillance for contact with Dutch secret agents. He had said of the Civil War: 'I think the Cause was too good to have fought for', and he felt that men should have trusted the king, but he placed constitutional liberties above the sanctity of a monarchy which he saw as presiding over a corrupt court and dangerously subject to Catholic influence.

While the turmoil of the times is most directly addressed in his prose works, its influence can be felt as an underlying current to the themes of his poetry, which was not published until after his death. Though his poetry was admired by a few other creative writers in the intervening years, its quality was not fully recognized until the 1920s, in particular by T.S. Eliot. John Aubrey defined something of Marvell's character when he wrote: 'He was in his conversation very modest, and of very few words, and though he loved wine he would never drink hard in company, and was wont to say that he would not play the good-fellow in any man's company in whose hands he would not trust his life.' Perhaps a wise stance, in the times in which he lived.

On a Drop of Dew

In this poem, Marvell draws on a traditional analogy between manna, dew and divine grace, and the concept that the individual soul was a part of a greater, divine element, to which it aspires.

> How does Marvell develop his theme idea through the use of verbs implying movement?

1   *orient* – orient pearls came from the Indian Ocean: the implication is that the dew is pearl-like.

3   *blowing* – blossoming.

5   *for* – here, this means 'because of'.

5–8   *For the clear region ... native element* – the idea is that the dew-drop encloses in itself the essence of the place it came from, which is heaven.

9   *slight* – spurn, reject.

19   *so* – here, this means 'thus', as in 'just so'.

23   *swart* – dark, black.

26   *a heaven less* – a lesser heaven.

27   *In how coy a figure wound* – wound, or enclosed, in such a modest shape.

29   *So the world excluding round* – Thus shutting out the world.

34   *girt* – clothed, ready to act.

On a Drop of Dew

See how the orient dew,
Shed from the bosom of the morn
  Into the blowing roses,
Yet careless of its mansion new,
5 For the clear region where 'twas born,
    Round in its self encloses,
    And in its little globe's extent,
  Frames as it can its native element.
  How it the purple flower does slight,
10   Scarce touching where it lies,
But gazing back upon the skies,
  Shines with a mournful light;
    Like its own tear,
Because so long divided from the sphere.
15   Restless it rolls and insecure
    Trembling lest it grow impure:
Till the warm sun pities its pain,
And to the skies exhale it back again.
    So the soul, that drop, that ray
20 Of the clear fountain of eternal day,
Could it within the human flower be seen,
    Remembering still its former height,
    Shuns the swart leaves and blossoms green;
  And, recollecting its own light,
25 Does, in its pure and circling thoughts, express
The greater heaven in a heaven less.
    In how coy a figure wound
    Every way it turns away:
  So the world excluding round,
30   Yet receiving in the day,
    Dark beneath, but bright above:
    Here disdaining, there in love,
  How loose and easy hence to go:
  How girt and ready to ascend.

37–40 *Such did … almighty sun* – The reference is to the feeding of the
children of Israel in the wilderness, after Moses led them from
captivity in Egypt. The account can be found in the Old Testament,
Exodus 16: '… when the dew that lay had gone up, behold, upon
the face of the wilderness there lay a small round thing, as small as
the hoar frost on the ground. And when the children of Israel saw
it, they said one to another, It is manna … and Moses said unto
them, This is the bread which the Lord hath given you to eat … and
when the sun waxed hot, it melted.'

Bermudas

In 1653, Marvell lived in the house of John Oxenbridge, who twice visisted
the Bermudas, which had been discovered by Juan Bermudez in 1515. They
were popularly regarded as a paradisial region, and Cromwell sent a fleet to
the colony to attempt to convert its inhabitants to Puritanism.

*Note the effect of the structure (octosyllabic couplets) and the metrical
patterns used by Marvell in this poem.*

  1 *ride* – as a ship rides at anchor.
  9 *wracks* – wrecks, or leaves stranded on the shore. The 'sea
     monsters' were probably whales.
 12 *prelate* – priest. The line possibly contains the idea of the missionary
     crew falling into the hands of Catholics.

 19 *close* – enclose.
 20 *Ormus* – a town at the end of the Persian Gulf, fabled for its wealth.

 23 *apples* – these were probably pineapples, which had to be replanted
     annually.

35   Moving but on a point below,
      It all about does upwards bend.
    Such did the manna's sacred dew distil,
    White and entire, though congealed and chill.
    Congealed on earth: but does, dissolving, run
40 Into the glories of the almighty sun.

Bermudas

    Where the remote Bermudas ride
    In the ocean's bosom unespied,
    From a small boat, that rowed along
    The list'ning winds received this song.
5   What should we do but sing his praise
    That led us through the watery maze,
    Unto an isle so long unknown,
    And yet far kinder than our own?
    Where he the huge sea-monsters wracks,
10 That lift the deep upon their backs,
    He lands us on a grassy stage,
    Safe from the storms, and prelate's rage.
    He gave us this eternal spring,
    Which here enamels everything,
15 And sends the fowls to us in care,
    On daily visits through the air.
    He hangs in shades the orange bright,
    Like golden lamps in a green night,
    And does in the pom'granates close
20 Jewels more rich than Ormus shows.
    He makes the figs our mouths to meet,
    And throws the melons at our feet,
    But apples plants of such a price,
    No tree could ever bear them twice.
25 With cedars, chosen by his hand,
    From Lebanon, he stores the land,
    And makes the hollow seas, that roar,

28   *ambergris* – a natural solid substance manufactured by certain
      species of whale. It is sometimes found cast up on shore, and was
      formerly greatly prized as a fixative in perfume-making.

The Nymph complaining for the death of her Fawn

There is an extensive tradition of poems mourning the death of animals.
Here, Marvell links the death of the fawn with the speaker's experience of
betrayal in love.

*How does Marvell create an impression of purity, and innocence betrayed,
through the language of the poem?*

3–4   *They cannot thrive/To kill thee ...* – they cannot profit from killing
      you.

17   *deodands* – if someone's personal possession (including animals)
      caused the death of a human, it was forfeit to the Crown. It was
      then sold and the money raised used for pious purposes. This was a
      deodand. The idea here is that this should apply equally to men who
      kill animals for no good reason.

Proclaim the ambergris on shore.
He cast (of which we rather boast)
30 The gospel's pearl upon our coast,
And in these rocks for us did frame
A temple, where to sound his name.
Oh let our voice his praise exalt,
Till it arrive at heaven's vault:
35 Which thence (perhaps) rebounding, may
Echo beyond the Mexique Bay.
Thus sung they, in the English boat,
A holy and a cheerful note,
And all the way, to guide their chime,
40 With falling oars they kept the time.

The Nymph complaining for the death of her Fawn

The wanton troopers riding by
Have shot my fawn, and it will die.
Ungentle men! They cannot thrive
To kill thee. Thou ne'er didst alive
5 Them any harm: alas, nor could
Thy death yet do them any good.
I'm sure I never wished them ill;
Nor do I for all this; nor will:
But if my simple prayers may yet
10 Prevail with heaven to forget
Thy murder, I will join my tears
Rather than fail. But, O my fears!
It cannot die so. Heaven's King
Keeps register of everything:
15 And nothing may we use in vain.
E'en beasts must be with justice slain,
Else men are made their deodands.
Though they should wash their guilty hands
In this warm life-blood, which doth part

24 *offer for their sin* – ironically, the troopers have killed the only thing whose innocent purity could be offered in expiation of their sin. Though the poem does not sustain an allegory, there are allusions throughout to Biblical passages (especially in lines 71–92, which contain echoes of the *Song of Solomon*), and the diction focuses on concepts of purity and death, raising ideas of sacrifice. However, a stress on this aspect of the poem would provide a reading which set aside what the poem is saying about innocence and the betrayal of trust, which, through the voice of the nymph, seems to be communicated very clearly.

26 *counterfeit* – false.

32 *dear* – used punningly: see also 'heart' in line 36.

20   From thine, and wound me to the heart,
     Yet could they not be clean: their stain
     Is dyed in such a purple grain.
     There is not such another in
     The world, to offer for their sin.
25   Unconstant Sylvio, when yet
     I had not found him counterfeit,
     One morning (I remember well)
     Tied in this silver chain and bell,
     Gave it to me: nay, and I know
30   What he said then; I'm sure I do.
     Said he, Look how your huntsman here
     Hath taught a fawn to hunt his dear.
     But Sylvio soon had me beguiled.
     This waxed tame, while he grew wild,
35   And quite regardless of my smart,
     Left me his fawn, but took his heart.
      Thenceforth I set myself to play
     My solitary time away
     With this: and very well content,
40   Could so mine idle life have spent.
     For it was full of sport; and light
     Of foot, and heart; and did invite
     Me to its game; it seemed to bless
     Itself in me. How could I less
45   Than love it? O I cannot be
     Unkind, t'a beast that loved me.
      Had it lived long, I do not know
     Whether it too might have done so
     As Sylvio did: his gifts might be
50   Perhaps as false or more than he.
     But I am sure, for ought that I
     Could in so short a time espy,
     Thy love was far more better than
     The love of false and cruel men.
55   With sweetest milk, and sugar, first
     I it at mine own fingers nursed.
     And as it grew, so every day

70 *four* – pronounced as a disyllable, for the sake of the metre.

It waxed more white and sweet than they.
It had so sweet a breath! And oft
60 I blushed to see its foot more soft,
And white (shall I say than my hand?)
Nay, any lady's of the land.
    It is a wondrous thing, how fleet
'Twas on those little silver feet.
65 With what a pretty skipping grace,
It oft would challenge me the race:
And when 't had left me far away,
'Twould stay, and run again, and stay.
For it was nimbler much than hinds;
70 And trod, as on the four winds.
    I have a garden of my own
But so with roses overgrown,
And lilies, that you would it guess
To be a little wilderness.
75 And all the springtime of the year
It only loved to be there.
Among the beds of lilies, I
Have sought it oft, where it should lie;
Yet could not, till itself would rise,
80 Find it, although before mine eyes.
For, in the flaxen lilies' shade,
It like a bank of lilies laid.
Upon the roses it would feed,
Until its lips e'en seemed to bleed:
85 And then to me 'twould boldly trip,
And print those roses on my lip.
But all its chief delight was still
On roses thus itself to fill:
And its pure virgin limbs to fold
90 In whitest sheets of lilies cold.
Had it lived long, it would have been
Lilies without, roses within.
    O help! O help! I see it faint:
And die as calmly as a saint.
95 See how it weeps. The tears do come

97 *balsam* – here, the tree which exudes the aromatic gum of the same name.

99 *Heliades* – the daughters of Helios, in Greek mythology the sun god: their brother Phaeton died when he drove his father's chariot and could not control it. They were transformed into trees, and the tears which they wept into amber.

104 *Diana* – goddess of chastity and hunting, and thus eminently appropriate to the theme of the poem.

106 *turtles* – turtle-doves.

107 *Elysium* – the classical paradise.

110 *bespeak* – order to be made.

Sad, slowly dropping like a gum.
So weeps the wounded balsam: so
The holy frankincense doth flow.
The brotherless Heliades
100 Melt in such amber tears as these.
    I in a golden vial will
Keep these two crystal tears; and fill
It till it do o'erflow with mine;
Then place it in Diana's shrine.
105   Now my sweet fawn is vanished to
Whither the swans and turtles go:
In fair Elysium to endure,
With milk-white lambs, and ermines pure.
O do not run too fast: for I
110 Will but bespeak thy grave, and die.
    First my unhappy statue shall
Be cut in marble; and withal,
Let it be weeping too: but there
The engraver sure his art may spare,
115 For I so truly thee bemoan,
That I shall weep though I be stone:
Until my tears, still dropping, wear
My breast, themselves engraving there.
There at my feet shalt thou be laid,
120 Of purest alabaster made:
For I would have thine image be
White as I can, though not as thee.

The Definition of Love

The theme of this poem seems to be less a definition of love than a statement of acceptance of despair as more noble than hope in a doomed relationship. The theme is developed through a series of conceits which depend initially on the use of abstract nouns as personifications. It sets the lovers and their experience within a cosmic context.

> The poem is full of echoes of ideas which can be found in other poems by Marvell, and in the work of other metaphysical poets. Which are immediately noticeable?

8   *tinsel* – glittering with superficial brilliance.

10   *extended soul* – his soul resides in his mistress, no longer within him.

17–20   *And therefore ... embraced* – the complex idea in these lines has connotations both of the wheel of Fortune (Fate) and of the earth spinning between the poles.

24   *planisphere* – an instrument on which plane surfaces move against each other, acting as a celestial globe. It is also known as an astrolabe. The idea in this stanza is of the total upheaval of earth and the heavens, upsetting the existing natural order which, according to Marvell's argument here, is keeping the lovers apart.

31–2   *conjunction/opposition* – astrological terms, used to show that, despite the lovers' close mental or spiritual union, the stars, controlling their destinies, oppose their physical conjunction.

The Definition of Love

My Love is of a birth as rare
As 'tis for object strange and high:
It was begotten by Despair
Upon Impossibility.

5 Magnanimous Despair alone
Could show me so divine a thing,
Where feeble Hope could ne'er have flown
But vainly flapped its tinsel wing.

And yet I quickly might arrive
10 Where my extended Soul is fixt,
But Fate does iron wedges drive,
And always crowds itself betwixt.

For Fate with jealous eye does see
Two perfect Loves; nor lets them close:
15 Their union would her ruin be,
And her tyrannic power depose.

And therefore her decrees of steel
Us at the distant Poles have placed,
(Though Love's whole World on us doth wheel)
20 Not by themselves to be embraced,

Unless the giddy Heaven fall,
And Earth some new convulsion tear;
And, us to join, the World should all
Be cramped into a planisphere.

25 As lines (so Loves) oblique may well
Themselves in every angle greet:
But ours so truly parallel,
Though infinite, can never meet.

Therefore the Love which us doth bind,
30 But Fate so enviously debars,
Is the conjunction of the Mind,
And opposition of the Stars.

To his Coy Mistress

This poem draws on an ancient lyric tradition – *carpe diem* or 'seize the day'.

Note how the tone changes as the persuasive argument progresses.

5–7   *Ganges ... Humber* – a witty rhetorical linking of the exotic Indian river with Marvell's local one: he came from Hull.

8   *ten years before the flood* – near the beginning of known time.

10   *conversion of the Jews* – this was expected to happen in the last days, at the end of time.

11   *vegetable love* – in the order of nature, the vegetable kingdom was above stones and below animals: vegetables had only two powers, growth and reproduction.

13–18   *A hundred years ... heart* – a conventional hyperbolic catalogue of the mistress's charms.

22   *Time's winged chariot* – the figure of personified Time is sometimes shown with wings, sometimes shown in a chariot. Marvell has conflated the image here.

27   *try* – assail.

29   *quaint honour* – Marvell's pun here has a long tradition: 'quaint' was used by writers as far back as Chaucer in the fourteenth century to refer to the female pudenda. The colloquial euphemism 'honour' was also sometimes used.

36   *instant fires* – whatever the lady may say, her body is clearly sexually aroused.

To his Coy Mistress

Had we but world enough, and time,
This coyness, lady, were no crime.
We would sit down, and think which way
To talk, and pass our long love's day.
5   Thou by the Indian Ganges' side
Should'st rubies find: I by the tide
Of Humber would complain. I would
Love you ten years before the flood:
And you should, if you please, refuse,
10   Till the conversion of the Jews.
My vegetable love should grow
Vaster than empires, and more slow.
A hundred years should go to praise
Thine eyes, and on thy forehead gaze.
15   Two hundred to adore each breast:
But thirty thousand to the rest.
An age at least to every part,
And the last age should show your heart:
For, lady, you deserve this state;
20   Nor would I love at lower rate.
    But at my back I always hear
Time's winged chariot hurrying near:
And yonder all before us lie
Deserts of vast eternity.
25   Thy beauty shall no more be found;
Nor, in thy marble vault, shall sound
My echoing song: there worms shall try
That long-preserved virginity:
And your quaint honour turn to dust;
30   And into ashes all my lust.
The grave's a fine and private place,
But none, I think, do there embrace.
    Now, therefore, while the youthful hue
Sits on thy skin like morning dew,
35   And while thy willing soul transpires
At every pore with instant fires,

40   *slow-chapped* – 'chaps' are jaws. The image of a slowly-chewing jaw is a particularly powerful conceit, coming shortly after the graveyard imagery.

41–4   *Let us roll ... iron gates of life* – This series of images. combining the abstact with the concrete, seems to work by triggering sensations in the reader's mind, rather than by exact analogy. The force of the diction ('tear', 'rough') seems to suggest that the mistress is a virgin, and that the sexual encounter will be a deflowering.

45–46   *sun ... run* – the last couplet is a final, assured conjunction of the images of time and sexuality on which the poem is built. 'Sun' is used punningly.

The Fair Singer

The theme of the enchantment cast by a woman singing has been used by many poets, and was popular with Marvell's contemporaries. It has its roots in classical myth; in Homer's *Odyssey* the Sirens lured sailors to their deaths through song.

> *How do you respond to this image of woman as enemy and enchantress, man as defenceless victim?*

9,18   – 'curled' and 'gained' are disyllables.

Now let us sport us while we may;
And now, like amorous birds of prey,
Rather at once our time devour,
40 Than languish in his slow-chapped power.
Let us roll all our strength, and all
Our sweetness, up into one ball:
And tear our pleasures with rough strife,
Thorough the iron gates of life.
45 Thus, though we cannot make our sun
Stand still, yet we will make him run.

The Fair Singer

To make a final conquest of all me,
Love did compose so sweet an enemy,
In whom both beauties to my death agree,
Joining themselves in fatal harmony;
5 That while she with her eyes my heart does bind,
She with her voice might captivate my mind.

I could have fled from one but singly fair:
My disentangled soul itself might save,
Breaking the curled trammels of her hair;
10 But how should I avoid to be her slave,
Whose subtle art invisibly can wreathe
My fetters of the very air I breathe?

It had been easy fighting in some plain,
Where victory might hang in equal choice,
15 But all resistance against her is vain,
Who has th'advantage both of eyes and voice,
And all my forces needs must be undone
She having gained both the wind and sun.

The Picture of Little T.C. in a Prospect of Flowers

The subject of this poem is thought to be Theophila Cornewall, who was born in 1644. Her elder sibling, also called Theophila, had died at the age of two days in 1643. At the opening of this poem, Marvell presents a strongly visual picture of a pure child in an idyllic setting, but note how the language he uses is drawn from warfare, as it is in some of his poems dealing with mature sexual love.

> *What warnings for the future are implicit in the poem?*

5   *gives them names* – as Adam named things in Eden. There is a sense of 'before the Fall' here.

6   *roses* – in Christian symbolism, roses stand for incorruptibility.

10   *darling of the gods* – Theophila means 'loved by the gods'. This stanza seems to suggest that she will conquer erotic Love (Cupid).

14   *ensigns* – banners.

16   *virtuous enemy* – this is an oxymoron, a figure of speech in which two opposing ideas are linked to produce a new idea: many metaphysical conceits depend on this technique.

17   *in time compound* – make a settlement (e.g. of a dispute) in good time.

18   *parley* – discuss terms or make a treaty, another military, or diplomatic, expression.

22   *but* – only.

The Picture of Little T.C. in a Prospect of Flowers

See with what simplicity
This nymph begins her golden days!
In the green grass she loves to lie,
And there with her fair aspect tames
5   The wilder flowers, and gives them names:
But only with the roses plays;
        And them does tell
What colour best becomes them, and what smell.

Who can foretell for what high cause
10 This darling of the gods was born!
Yet this is she whose chaster laws
The wanton Love shall one day fear,
And, under her command severe,
See his bow broke and ensigns torn.
15   Happy, who can
Appease this virtuous enemy of man!

O, then let me in time compound,
And parley with those conquering eyes;
Ere they have tried their force to wound,
20 Ere, with their glancing wheels, they drive
In triumph over hearts that strive,
And them that yield but more despise.
        Let me be laid,
Where I may see thy glories from some shade.

25 Meantime, whilst every verdant thing
Itself does at thy beauty charm,
Reform the errors of the spring;
Make that the tulips may have share
Of sweetness, seeing they are fair;
30 And roses of their thorns disarm:
        But most procure
That violets may a longer age endure.

36   *Flora* – the Roman goddess of flowers, associated with the spring.

The Garden

The prelapsarian (before the Fall of Man) theme which Marvell touched on in *The Picture of Little T.C. in a Prospect of Flowers* is dominant throughout this poem. The poet places himself, like Adam, alone in the garden, which is full of delights. His only duty is to contemplate them. The poem exploits the antithesis between the busyness of the world and its temptations, sexual pleasure and temporal achievement, and the sensual but innocent delights which the garden offers to the solitary man: it moves through contemplation of the aspiring soul to return to the joys of the garden itself.

> To what extent is it necessary to understand the philosophical ideas behind this poem to be able to enjoy it? Does a reading of it depend on the knowledge that the reader already has, or can it be fully enjoyed on a different level?

    1   *vainly* – futilely, or arrogantly.

    2   *the palm, the oak, the bays* – these reward victory in war, statesmanship and poetry.

    6   *upbraid* – scold, or plait together.

    7   *close* – draw together.

13–14   *your sacred plants ... will grow* – this refers back to the palm, oak and bays, and suggests here that they are nothing special in the context of the garden as a whole.

   15   *rude* – unpolished, rough. Marvell uses a paradox here: the more usual idea is that it is society that is 'polished'.

   17   *white/red* – traditionally, these colours symbolized beauty in women.

   18   *amorous* – worthy of love, or, itself seductive.

But, O young beauty of the woods
Whom Nature courts with fruits and flowers,
35 Gather the flowers, but spare the buds;
Lest Flora angry at thy crime,
To kill her infants in their prime,
Do quickly make th'example yours;
                    And, ere we see,
40 Nip in the blossom all our hopes and thee.

The Garden

How vainly men themselves amaze
To win the palm, the oak, or bays,
And their uncessant labours see
Crowned from some single herb or tree,
5 Whose short and narrow vergèd shade
Does prudently their toils upbraid;
While all flowers and all trees do close
To weave the garlands of repose

Fair Quiet, have I found thee here,
10 And Innocence, thy sister dear!
Mistaken long, I sought you then
In busy companies of men.
Your sacred plants, if here below,
Only among the plants will grow.
15 Society is all but rude,
To this delicious solitude.

No white nor red was ever seen
So amorous as this lovely green.
Fond lovers, cruel as their flame,
20 Cut in these trees their mistress' name.
Little, alas, they know, or heed,
How far these beauties hers exceed!
Fair trees! wheres'e'er your barks I wound,
No name shall but your own be found.

29–32 *Apollo … reed* – in classical mythology, many of those whom the
gods sought to seduce were changed into trees or plants. Two such
cases are referred to in this stanza.

33–34 *What wondrous … grass* – the poet appears to be actively seduced
by the fruits, but his fall (unlike Adam's) is harmless.

41 *from pleasure less* – this is a turning-point in the poem: the mind
desires different things than those sensual delights which satisfy the
body.

43–6 *The mind … seas* – these lines draw on the idea that the sea holds a
parallel creation to that on earth.

44 *straight* – immediately.

46 *…other seas* – the mind is capable of creating imaginary forms.

47–48 *Annihilating … green shade* – these lines have been interpreted in
different ways. In their context, a straightforward explanation of
what Marvell is suggesting might be that the mind of the solitary
poet can imaginatively wipe out the whole of creation, reducing it to
his immediate moment of experience.

49 *sliding foot* – it is the man's foot that slides.

54 *whets* – preens.

55–6 *And … light* – these lines draw on Platonic theory; the soul rests,
like a bird on a branch, between heaven, to which it aspires, and
earth. ' Various light' refers to the colours that light assumes in the
created world, less pure than the white light of eternity.

25   When we have run our passion's heat,
      Love hither makes his best retreat.
      The gods, that mortal beauty chase,
      Still in a tree did end their race.
      Apollo hunted Daphne so,
30   Only that she might laurel grow.
      And Pan did after Syrinx speed,
      Nor as a nymph, but for a reed.

      What wondrous life in this I lead!
      Ripe apples drop about my head;
35   The luscious clusters of the vine
      Upon my mouth do crush their wine;
      The nectarine, and curious peach,
      Into my hands themselves do reach;
      Stumbling on melons, as I pass,
40   Ensnared with flowers, I fall on grass.

      Meanwhile the mind, from pleasure less,
      Withdraws into its happiness:
      The mind, that ocean where each kind
      Does straight its own resemblance find,
45   Yet it creates, transcending these,
      Far other worlds, and other seas;
      Annihilating all that's made
      To a green thought in a green shade.

      Here at the fountain's sliding foot,
50   Or at some fruit-tree's mossy root,
      Casting the body's vest aside,
      My soul into the boughs does glide:
      There like a bird it sits, and sings,
      Then whets, and combs its silver wings;
55   And, till prepared for longer flight,
      Waves in its plumes the various light.

58   *without a mate* – as Adam was, before the creation of Eve.

60   *meet* – Genesis 1:18. God made a 'help meet' for Adam.

61–4 Man was not given the opportunity to enjoy paradise alone; that
      would have been a double blessing!

66   *dial* – sundial. This could either refer metaphorically to the garden
      as a whole, laid out with beds and borders reflecting the passage of
      the sun, or it could be a floral sundial.

68   *Does ... run* – the sunlight is filtered through the trees, and is
      therefore weakened.

70   *time* – a pun: the herb 'thyme' is brought to mind, as it is much
      beloved by bees.

Such was that happy garden-state
While man there walked without a mate:
After a place so pure, and sweet
60 What other help could yet be meet!
But 'twas beyond a mortal's share
To wander solitary there:
Two paradises 'twere in one
To live in paradise alone.

65 How well the skilful gardener drew
Of flowers and herbs this dial new,
Where from above the milder sun
Does through a fragrant zodiac run;
And, as it works, th'industrious bee
70 Computes its time as well as we.
How could such sweet and wholesome hours
Be reckoned but with herbs and flowers!

An Horatian Ode upon Cromwell's Return from Ireland

This poem has baffled many commentators. Where did Marvell's sympathies lie? He was an employee of the Parliamentarian general, Lord Fairfax, which indicates some commitment to the Commonwealth. It is worth noting, however, that Fairfax was himself opposed to the execution of King Charles. The poem was, it seems, originally popular with the Royalists, though it was excluded from all save two of the 1681 editions of Marvell's poetry. Undoubtedly, the section of the poem which is most remembered by general readers, quoted and anthologized, is the mid-section, concerning the execution of the king. The terms in which Charles is described compare strangely with some of the language used to describe Cromwell. Is it, perhaps, best to consider this poem as politically expedient, written at a time of social and philosophical uncertainties, and regard its complexities as an accurate reflection of the way in which many people may have felt at the time?

The poem was most likely written between May 1650, when Cromwell returned from Ireland, and June of that year, when he began his campaign against Scotland. The Scots had not initiated hostilities, and Fairfax resigned as Commander in Chief of the army because he felt this pre-emptive action was morally wrong. King Charles I had been executed in Whitehall in January 1649.

An ode was, in classical literature, a poem intended for singing, often in the form of an address. Horace's *Odes* imitated earlier Greek models, and some of his writing celebrated the restoration of order after the Roman civil wars. Marvell's poetic form here is original, but some of the detail of the ode is based on the epic poetry of another Roman poet, Lucan.

1–8   *The forward youth ... hall* – the opening lines suggest that a young man who wishes to advance in such times should abandon poetry and take up arms.

15–16   *Did ... divide* – this suggests that Cromwell burst through the ranks of the Parliamentarians as lightning splits a cloud, which is the body in which it dwells.

18   *emulous* – those who would imitate.

19–20   *And with such ... oppose* – it is worse to try to pen in such men than to oppose them.

23–4   *And Caesar's ... blast* – laurels were thought to be proof against lightning. Julius Caesar, crowned with laurels, was not immune to insurrection, and was assassinated by Brutus, Cassius and their fellow conspirators. Likewise, Charles I fell to Cromwell and the Parliamentarians.

An Horatian Ode upon Cromwell's Return from Ireland

The forward youth that would appear
Must now forsake his muses dear,
 Nor in the shadows sing
 His numbers languishing.
5 'Tis time to leave the books in dust,
And oil the unused armour's rust:
 Removing from the wall
 The corslet of the hall.
So restless Cromwell could not cease
10 In the inglorious arts of peace,
 But through adventurous war
 Urged his active star.
And, like the three-forked lightning, first
Breaking the clouds where it was nursed,
15 Did thorough his own side
 His fiery way divide.
For 'tis all one to courage high
The emulous or enemy:
 And with such to enclose
20 Is more than to oppose.
Then burning through the air he went,
And palaces and temples rent:
 And Caesar's head at last
 Did through his laurels blast.

27–40   *And, if ... or weak* – the tone of these lines is ambivalent. The conditionals ('if') seem to detract from any praise which Marvell is giving to Cromwell.

32   *bergamot* – this is the name of an aromatic herb, and also a variety of pear, known as the prince's pear. It is likely that the second definition is intended here.

38   *ancient rights* – at his trial, Charles asked how anyone could claim his life or his possessions as his own if those who had no right to power made new laws, and withdrew the fundamental laws of the country.

41–2   *Nature ... less* – Nature abhors a vacuum, but an even greater abhorrence is 'penetration', the occupation of one space by two bodies at the same time.

46   *deepest scars* – refers to scars given *by* Cromwell.

47–52   *And Hampton ... case* – these lines refer to the king's flight from Hampton Court to Carisbrooke, on the Isle of Wight, where the governor of the castle treated him as a prisoner. Marvell seems to suggest that this flight may have been engineered by an unproven contemporary rumour.

52   *case* – plight or prison.

53–64   *That thence ...* The focus shifts here to Charles. Marvell presents the execution as a theatrical event. Charles was beheaded on a scaffold, or stage, outside the Banqueting House in Whitehall. It seems that the soldiers who were on duty at the beheading were instructed to clap to drown the king's speech. There is an underlying irony to the theatrical imagery; Charles had himself acted in masques within the building outside which he died.

59–60   *keener eye ... try* – Charles's eye was keener, or sharper, than the axe. In Latin, *acies* means both 'eyesight' and 'blade': a complex classical pun.

25 'Tis madness to resist or blame
The force of angry heaven's flame:
    And, if we would speak true,
    Much to the man is due,
Who, from his private gardens, where
30 He lived reserved and austere,
    As if his highest plot
    To plant the bergamot,
Could by industrious valour climb
To ruin the great work of time,
35 And cast the kingdom old
    Into another mould.
Though justice against fate complain,
And plead the ancient rights in vain:
    But those do hold or break
40 As men are strong or weak.
Nature, that hateth emptiness,
Allows of penetration less:
    And therefore must make room
    Where greater spirits come.
45 What field of all the Civil Wars,
Where his were not the deepest scars?
    And Hampton shows what part
    He had of wiser art,
Where, twining subtile fears with hope,
50 He wove a net of such a scope,
    That Charles himself might chase
    To Carisbrooke's narrow case:
That thence the royal actor borne
The tragic scaffold might adorn:
55 While round the armed bands
    Did clap their bloody hands.
He nothing common did or mean
Upon that memorable scene:
    But with his keener eye
60 The axe's edge did try:

61–4   *Nor called ... bed* – eyewitnesses of the execution remarked on the king's calmness and dignity.

66   *forced* – a disyllable, meaning here taken by force. The focus of the poem has now shifted back to Cromwell.

68–72   *Capitol ... fate* – a reference to the finding of a preserved human head when the foundations of the temple of Jupiter Capitolium were dug in Rome. This was seen as a good omen. *Caput*, in Latin, means head.

74   *one year* – the Irish campaign lasted approximately ten months.

76   *act and know* – Cromwell is described as a man of action and of thought.

77–80   *They ... trust* – an questionable assertion. The Irish war was a bloody and violent campaign.

82   *still* – always, or up to now: the ambiguity may be deliberate.

87   *what he may* – as far as he can.

95   *lure* – a lure is made from feathers, and a hawk is trained to come to it. Here, it is used as a verb.

Nor called the gods with vulgar spite
To vindicate his helpless right,
    But bowed his comely head
    Down as upon a bed.
65 That was that memorable hour
Which first assured the forced power.
    So when they did design
    The Capitol's first line,
A bleeding head where they begun,
70 Did fright the architects to run;
    And yet in that the State
    Foresaw its happy fate.
And now the Irish are ashamed
To see themselves in one year tamed:
75   So much one man can do,
    That does both act and know.
They can affirm his praises best,
And have, though overcome, confessed
    How good he is, how just,
80   And fit for highest trust:
Nor yet grown stiffer with command,
But still in the Republic's hand:
    How fit he is to sway
    That can so well obey.
85 He to the Commons' feet presents
A kingdom, for his first year's rents:
    And, what he may, forbears
    His fame, it make it theirs:
And has his sword and spoils ungirt,
90 To lay them at the public's skirt.
    So when the falcon high
    Falls heavy from the sky,
She, having killed, no more does search
But on the next green bough to perch,
95   Where, when he first does lure,
    The falconer has her sure.
What may not then our isle presume
While Victory his crest does plume!

101–2　*A Caesar ... –* Marvell resumes the classical heroic parallels. Julius Caesar was conquerer of Gaul (France); Hannibal, a war leader from North Africa, marched on Rome.

104　*climacteric –* critical, bringing in a new epoch.

105　*Pict –* member of a Scottish tribe.

106　*parti-coloured –* variously coloured. In Latin, *pictum* means 'painted'. This is another classical pun. The Scots were regarded as turncoats and traitors.

107　*sad –* serious.

110　*mistake –* his colouring camouflages him.

117–18　*fright ... night –* the cross-hilt of a sword, being cruciform, was believed to have power over evil spirits.

How does the section describing the execution of the King relate to the rest of the poem?

What may not others fear
100   If thus he crown each year!
A Caesar he, ere long to Gaul,
To Italy a Hannibal,
    And to all states not free
Shall climacteric be.
105   The Pict no shelter now shall find
Within his parti-coloured mind;
    But from this valour sad
    Shrink underneath the plaid:
Happy if in the tufted brake
110   The English hunter him mistake,
    Nor lay his hounds in near
    The Caledonian deer.
But thou, the Wars' and Fortune's son,
March indefatigably on;
115   And for the last effect
    Still keep thy sword erect:
Besides the force it has to fright
The spirits of the shady night,
    The same arts that did gain
120   A power, must it maintain.

Henry Vaughan (1621 – 1695)

Henry Vaughan, his twin brother, Thomas, and their younger brother, William, were the sons of a Welsh gentleman, Thomas Vaughan of Tretower, whose family home was at Drenewydd (Newtown), Breconshire. The brothers were tutored locally, and in May 1638 Thomas went to Jesus College, Oxford, and it is likely that Henry was there as well. Henry Vaughan's youth is not well recorded: he may have studied law in London, and also have been attached to the 'tribe of Ben', followers of the poet Ben Jonson. However, he did not spend long in London, returning to Breconshire at the outbreak of the Civil War.

The Vaughan family was royalist, and it is possible that Henry fought on the King's side. Devoted to the Church of England, and losing many of his friends in the Civil War, the turmoil of the age had a profound effect on Henry Vaughan, both as a poet and in his personal life. The early death of his youngest brother also brought him grief. He never returned to London, but settled in Breconshire, eventually becoming a country physician. He married twice: his second wife was the sister of his first, and each bore him a son and two daughters.

Vaughan's early poetry is competent but less than heartfelt. It follows the conventions of secular love poetry, using the style of the time efficiently but without originality or much evidence of a personal voice. The turning-point in his poetic life appears to have been the influence of George Herbert (another poet whose family had strong Welsh connections). Vaughan revered Herbert both as a Christian and as a poet, referring to him as 'the blessed man ... whose holy life and verse gained many pious converts, (of whom I am the least)'. There are many echoes of Herbert's poems in those of Vaughan, in titles, subject-matter and images, but Vaughan's poetic voice is entirely his own. His poetry retains many of the verse structures and poetic techniques from his early, secular, writing which followed the practices of the Jonsonian school, and these two influences produce highly individual work; his poetry is truly metaphysical in its fusion of thought, feeling and language, and the use of reason to progress an exploration of experience.

Above all, Vaughan is a mystic poet, who strives in his writing to express his inner convictions and spiritual experiences. Both he and his brother Thomas investigated and published works on magic and mysticism, exploring hermetic philosophy which was based on the reinterpretation of pagan mysteries, which dominated much renaissance culture, and which was still influential in the seventeenth century. Concepts from such sources underlie many of Vaughan's poems: the spiritual nature of light and darkness; the relationship between outward appearance and inner truth; the ubiquitous nature of God – all are explored in poems which are never dry debate, but often a paean of praise expressed in images of nature, drawn from the countryside in which Vaughan lived. These images are not simply decorative: they carry the poet's conviction that God is revealed through His creation, and that this revelation is afforded to one who observes with the clarity and simplicity of a child.

There is a further aspect to Vaughan's writing, which should not be overlooked. He was, essentially, a Welsh poet writing in English. He called himself 'Silurist': the Silures were a British tribe at the time of the Roman occupation, living in what became Wales. It is probable that Vaughan was himself Welsh-speaking: in any event, he is likely to have heard the language spoken every day. The lyrical flow of Vaughan's lines, the rich accumulation of images and sounds which engage the ear as well as the intellect, echo the forms and cadences of the Welsh language. Another element in the richness of his verse is the fact that many of Vaughan's lines are based on Biblical texts, and it is no accident that the source is frequently the *Song of Solomon* or *Revelation*, both books which combine mystery and mysticism expressed in resonant language.

Vaughan first published his religious poetry in 1650, and these poems are both celebratory and exploratory. A second edition in 1655 incorporated a large number of new poems, and these are more sombre, with greater reliance on Biblical sources than his earlier work. They can be seen as looking towards death, though Vaughan lived to a good age, outliving his brother Thomas by 29 years. The selection of Vaughan's poems printed here draws on both editions: the first six are from the 1650 edition, the last three from that of 1655.

Regeneration

This is the opening poem after the dedication of **Silex Scintillans**. It is the natural starting-point for the collection, dealing with spiritual re-birth after the writer's rejection of a life dedicated to worldly pleasure. The poem moves thematically from images and references closely linked with the Old Testament to those of the New. The quotation which appears at the end is a combination of two verses of the *Song of Solomon* and can be explained by reference to the allegorical reading of that Old Testament love-song as figuring the mutual love between Christ and his Church.

Note the appeals to the senses which run throughout the poem.

1　*A ward, and still in bonds* ... – this introduces the theme of bondage to Old Testament law, and also the idea of being in the care of another, which is maintained over the first three stanzas.

4　*primrosed* – 'the primrose path to the everlasting bonfire', Shakespeare: *Macbeth* 2.3.

22　*late pains* – this may refer to Vaughan's experiences during the Civil War, and to his brother's death.

25–32　*With that ... God* – this stanza is an allegorical account of a 'calling' to a life dedicated to religion, away from the 'smoke' (1.23), the transitory pleasures of the world.

28　*Jacob's bed* – Genesis 29:1. The account of Jacob's journeys has him travelling east: 'he lighted upon a certain place, and tarried there all night, because the sun was set.' This was the place where Jacob dreamed of the ladder ascending into heaven, and of hearing the voice of God.

Regeneration

A ward, and still in bonds, one day
    I stole abroad;
It was high spring, and all the way
    Primrosed and hung with shade;
5   Yet was it frost within,
        And surly winds
Blasted my infant buds, and sin
    Like clouds eclipsed my mind.

Stormed thus, I straight perceived my spring
10   Mere stage and show,
My walk a monstrous, mountained thing,
    Rough-cast with rocks and snow;
    And as a pilgrim's eye
        Far from relief,
15 Measures the melancholy sky,
    Then drops, and rains for grief,

So sighed I upwards still; at last
        'Twixt steps and falls
I reached the pinnacle, where placed
20   I found a pair of scales;
I took them up and laid
        In th'one late pains;
The other smoke and pleasures weighed,
    But proved the heavier grains;

25 With that, some cried, *Away*! Straight I
        Obeyed, and led
Full east, a fair, fresh field could spy;
    Some called it Jacob's bed,
    A virgin soil which no
30   Rude feet ere trod,
Where (since he stepped there) only go
    Prophets, and friends of God.

33f. *Here, I reposed* ... – this, and the following stanzas, are an allegorical account of the state of grace which Vaughan sees himself entering as he turns his back on worldly pursuits.

41   *unthrift* – not thrifty, therefore generous.
     vital – life-giving.
43   *azure* – deep blue.

54   *cistern* – basin.
55   *divers stones* – I Peter 2:5: 'Ye also, as lively stones, are built up as a spiritual house ...'

60   *centre* – the earth. The image of the stones and their place seems to reflect medieval cosmology, in which the Earth was at the centre of the universe, and the heavens were beyond the furthest sphere. The dancing, lively stones are freed from their earthly fetters.

Here, I reposed; but scarce well set,
   A grove descried
35 Of stately height, whose branches met
    And mixed on every side;
   I entered, and once in,
     (Amazed to see 't,)
  Found all was changed, and a new spring
40 Did all my senses greet;

The unthrift sun shot vital gold,
   A thousand pieces,
And heaven its azure did unfold,
   Checkered with snowy fleeces;
45 The air was all in spice,
    And every bush
  A garland wore; thus fed my eyes,
   But all the ear lay hush.

Only a little fountain lent
50   Some use for ears,
And on the dumb shades language spent,
   The music of her tears;
   I drew her near, and found
    The cistern full
55 Of divers stones, some bright and round,
   Others ill-shaped and dull.

The first (pray mark) as quick as light
   Danced through the flood,
But, th' last, more heavy than the night,
60 Nailed to the centre stood;
   I wondered much, but tired
    At last with thought,
  My restless eye that still desired
   As strange an object brought;

68 *ray* – the sun's ray.

70 *a rushing wind* – Acts 2:2: 'And suddenly, there came a sound from heaven as of a rushing mighty wind …' This is the account of Pentecost, the coming of the Holy Spirit, the third person of the Trinity.

80 *Where I please* – John 3.8: 'The wind bloweth where it listeth.'

81–2 *Lord, then said I* … – Vaughan's request is to die as the old, unregenerated man, to be reborn in a state of grace. In the 'Emblem' – or foreword – to the 1650 edition of his poems, Vaughan states: 'In Dying, I have been born again …' This is a similar idea to that expressed by Herbert in lines 19–20 of *Aaron*.

The Retreat

This poem exemplifies Vaughan's vision of childhood as a time of purity and intrinsic understanding of spiritual truths. This attitude prefigures the work of the later poet, Wordsworth. The child is in harmony with nature, which is a reflection and expression of the will of the Creator. The title is deliberately ambiguous: a religious retreat is a withdrawing from the world, and the term also signifies a moving backwards.

4 *my second race* – Hebrews 12.1: 'Let us run with patience the race that is set before us.' In this poem, Vaughan draws on the Platonic concept of the pre-existence of souls.

5 *aught* – anything.

8 *my first love* – Revelation 2.4: ' . . thou has left thy first love.' This is the love of God, which Vaughan suggests is a natural human instinct.

65 It was a bank of flowers, where I descried,
       (Though 'twas midday,)
   Some fast asleep, others broad-eyed
       And taking in the ray;
       Here musing long, I heard
70   A rushing wind
   Which still increased, but whence it stirred
       No where I could not find;

   I turned me round, and to each shade
       Dispatched an eye
75 To see if any leaf had made
       Least motion, or reply,
       But while I list'ning sought
           My mind to ease
   By knowing where 'twas, or where not,
80   It whispered, *Where I please*.

   Lord, then said I, *on me one breath,*
   And let me die before my death!

   CANT. CAP. 4. VER. 17.
   Arise, O North, and come thou South-wind; and
   blow upon my garden, that the spices thereof may flow out.

The Retreat

       Happy those early days! when I
       Shined in my angel infancy;
       Before I understood this place
       Appointed for my second race,
   5   Or taught my soul to fancy aught
       But a white, celestial thought,
       When yet I had not walked above
       A mile, or two, from my first love,
       And looking back, (at the short space,)
   10 Could see a glimpse of his bright face;

11–14   *When on … eternity* – the natural world is a pale reflection of the glory of God; however, through it man can catch a glimpse of His splendour.

26   *city of palm trees* – Deuteronomy 34.4: 'Jericho, the city of palm trees.'

27–8   *But (ah!) … way* – neo-platonic philosophy can be seen behind these lines. Plato's *Phaedo* states: ' … the soul too is then dragged by the body into the region of the changeable … and she is like a drunkard …' Vaughan suggests that the longer he lives the more he loses contact with his primal innocence and spirituality.

Note the alliteration in lines 16 – 20, and consider its effect.

The Morning-watch

Much of the vocabulary of this celebratory poem draws on concepts of sound, music and singing. In what other ways is it song-like?

        Morning-watch – morning prayer.
10   *quick* – alive.

When on some gilded cloud or flower
My gazing soul would dwell an hour,
And in those weaker glories spy
Some shadows of eternity;
15 Before I taught my tongue to wound
My conscience with a sinful sound,
Or had the black art to dispense
A sev'ral sin to every sense,
But felt through all this fleshly dress
20 Bright shoots of everlastingness.
    Oh, how I long to travel back
And tread again that ancient track!
That I might once more reach that plain
Where first I left my glorious train,
25 From whence the enlightened spirit sees
That shady city of palm trees;
But (ah!) my soul with too much stay
Is drunk, and staggers in the way.
Some men a forward motion love,
30 But I by backward steps would move,
And when this dust falls to the urn
In that state I came, return.

The Morning-watch

O joys! Infinite sweetness! with what flowers,
And shoots of glory, my soul breaks, and buds!
      All the long hours
      Of night, and rest
5   Through the still shrouds
      Of sleep, and clouds,
  This dew fell on my breast;
    O how it bloods,
And spirits all my earth! hark! in what rings,
10 And hymning circulations the quick world
      Awakes, and sings;
      The rising winds,

22 *Whose echo is Heav'n's bliss* – the direct response to prayer is a faint echo of the joys of heaven.

The Dawning

This poem is more exploratory than *The Morning-watch*, though it draws on similar ideas. Here, Vaughan take on a more self-examining role.

> *Compare the images in the first verse paragraph with those in* The Morning-watch.

2 *The Bridegroom's coming!* – Matthew 25.6: 'Behold, the bridegroom cometh ...'

And falling springs,
Birds, beasts, all things
15   Adore him in their kinds.
Thus all is hurled
In sacred hymns, and order, the great chime
And symphony of nature. Prayer is
The world in tune,
20   A spirit-voice,
And vocal joys
Whose echo is Heav'n's bliss.
O let me climb
When I lie down! The pious soul by night
25 Is like a clouded star, whose beams though said
To shed their light
Under some cloud
Yet are above,
And shine, and move
30   Beyond that misty shroud.
So in my bed
That curtained grave, though sleep, like ashes, hide
My lamp, and life, both shall in thee abide.

The Dawning

Ah! what time wilt thou come? when shall that cry,
  The Bridegroom's coming, fill the sky?
Shall it in the evening run,
When our words and works are done?
5 Or will thy all-surprising light
     Break at midnight?
When either sleep or some dark pleasure
Possesseth mad man without measure;
Or shall these early fragrant hours
10   Unlock thy bowers?
And with their blush of light descry
Thy locks crowned with eternity;

21   *pursy* – puffy, corpulent.

24   *morning star* – Revelation 22.16: 'I am the root and the offspring of
       David, and the bright and morning star.'

27   *in the van* – in the front, the vanguard.

35–6 *And though … keeps untainted* – The idea is that flowing water of
       elemental purity is a link to a primal, pure source of life, which is
       untainted by the corruption of the world.

Indeed, it is the only time
That with thy glory doth best chime;
15 All now are stirring, ev'ry field
        Full hymns doth yield,
The whole creation shakes off night,
And for thy shadow looks the light;
Stars now vanish without number,
20 Sleepy planets set and slumber,
The pursy clouds disband and scatter,
All expect some sudden matter;
Not one beam triumphs, but from far
        That morning star.

25 Oh, at what time soever, Thou,
(Unknown to us) the heavens wilt bow,
And, with thy angels in the van,
Descend to judge poor careless man,
Grant, I may not like puddle lie
30 In a corrupt security,
Where, if a traveller water crave,
He finds it dead and in a grave;
But as this restless vocal spring
All day and night doth run and sing,
35 And though here born, yet is acquainted
Elsewhere, and flowing keeps untainted;
So let me all my busy age
In thy free services engage;
And though (while here) of force I must
40 Have commerce sometimes with poor dust,
And in my flesh, though vile and low,
As this doth in her channel, flow,
Yet let my course, my aim, my love,
And chief acquaintance be above;
45 So when that day and hour shall come
In which thyself will be the sun,
Thou'lt find me dressed and on my way,
Watching the break of thy great Day.

The World

This vision of a planet hurtling through space, carrying the burden of sinful man, is apocalyptic in tone, and its opening lines are probably known to many who have no knowledge of who wrote them. The opening stanza draws on the pre-Copernican concept of the univers as a series of spheres. Time is only applicable to the Earth: everything beneath the Moon is mutable, subject to time and change.

Vaughan draws on his own time for his list of human stereotypes. How relevant are they today?

8 *quaintest strain* – most ingenious song.

14 *his eyes did pore* – his eyesight was ruined by close observation.

23–5 Yet *digged the mole ... clutch his prey* – these lines evoke an idea in one of Herbert's poems, *Confession*:
  'Like moles within us, heave, and cast about:
  And till they foot, and clutch their prey ...'

27 *perjuries* – false oaths.

The World

I saw Eternity the other night
Like a great Ring of pure and endless light,
   All calm, as it was bright;
And round beneath it, Time, in hours, days, years,
5   Driven by the spheres,
Like a vast shadow moved, in which the world
   And all her train were hurled.
The doting lover in his quaintest strain
   Did there complain;
10 Near him, his lute, his fancy, and his flights,
   Wit's sour delights,
With gloves and knots, the silly snares of pleasure,
   Yet his dear treasure,
All scattered lay, while he his eyes did pore
15   Upon a flower.

The darksome statesman hung with weights and woe,
Like a thick midnight fog moved there so slow
   He did not stay, nor go;
Condemning thoughts (like sad eclipses) scowl
20   Upon his soul,
And clouds of crying witnesses without
   Pursued him with one shout.
Yet digged the mole, and lest his ways be found,
   Worked under ground,
25 Where he did clutch his prey, but one did see
   That policy,
Churches and altars fed him, perjuries
   Were gnats and flies,
It rained about him blood and tears, but he
30   Drank them as free.

The fearful miser on a heap of rust
Sat pining all his life there, did scarce trust
   His own hands with the dust,

37 *pelf* – treasure, riches.

38 *epicure* – one who lives to please his sensual needs.

44–5 *And poor ... victory* – another Herbertian echo, this time from *The Church Militant.*

46–7 *Yet some ... sing and weep* – this refers to Revelation 7.14: '... God shall wipe away all tears from their eyes' and 15.3 'And they sing the song of Moses ... and the song of the Lamb.'

51 *grots* – grottoes, i.e. caves.

56 *he* – i.e. the sun.

59–60 *This ring ... for his bride* – this alludes to the mystical marriage of Christ and his Church.

Man

This is another exploration of the nature of humanity and its relationship to the Creator.

> *How does the approach which Vaughan takes in this poem compare with that to be found in* The World?

Yet would not place one piece above, but lives
35   In fear of thieves.
    Thousands there were as frantic as himself,
        And hugged each one his pelf,
    The downright epicure placed Heav'n in sense,
        And scorned pretence;
40   While others, slipped into a wide excess,
        Said little less;
    The weaker sort slight, trivial wares enslave.
        Who think them brave,
    And poor, despisèd truth sat counting by
45   Their victory.

    Yet some, who all this while did weep and sing.
    And sing and weep, soared up into the Ring;
        But most would use no wing.
    O fools (said I) thus to prefer dark night
50   Before true light.
    To live in grots and caves, and hate the day
        Because it shows the way,
    The way which from this dead and dark abode
        Leads up to God,
55   A way where you might tread the sun, and abe
        More bright than he.
    But as I did their madness so discuss,
        One whispered thus:
    This ring the Bridegroom did for none provide,
        But for his bride.

Man

    Weighing the steadfastness and state
Of some mean things which here below reside,
Where birds like watchful clocks the noiseless date
    And intercourse of times divide;

9   *staidness* – orderliness.

10   *cleave* – hold fast.

12–14 *The birds nor sow ... dressed so fine* – Matthew 6.26, 28-9: 'Behold
       the fowls of the air for they sow not, neither do they reap ... yet
       your heavenly Father feedeth them ... Consider the lilies of the field
       ... even Solomon in all his glory was not arrayed like one of these.'

23   *wit* – intelligence.
       stones – lodestones, which have magnetic properties and were used
       in compasses, Here, Vaughan draws on the concept that humanity
       alone shares reason with divine beings (angels) and that stones are
       on the very lowest rung of the ladder of existence. In this
       comparison, he relegates people to a place below that of the stones
       when it comes to using their intelligence.

26-27 *Man is the shuttle ... looms* – The image is drawn from weaving.

Cock-crowing

In this poem, Henry Vaughan draws directly on the writings of his brother
Thomas, who explored hermetic philosophy. (*Note:* amongst his other
attributes, the god Hermes was a keeper and a revealer of secrets; a simple
explanation of the term 'hermetic' is that it deals with secret things,
understandable only by the initiated.) 'The Soul ... is guided in her operations
by a spiritual, metaphysical grain, a seed or glance of light ... descending from
the first Father of Lights. For though His full-eyed love shines on nothing but
man, yet everything in the world is in some measure directed for his
preservation by a spice or touch of the First Intellect.' (*Anima Magica
Abscondita*, 1650).

Trace this idea through the poem. How is it used to develop argument?

1   *Father of lights* – James 1.17: 'Every good gift ... cometh down from
     the Father of lights.'

5   Where bees at night get home and hive, and flowers
              Early, as well as late,
    Rise with the sun, and set in the same bowers;

    I would (said I) my God would give
    The staidness of these things to man! for these
10 To his divine appointments ever cleave,
     And no new business breaks their peace;
    The birds nor sow nor reap, yet sup and dine;
             The flowers without clothes live,
    Yet Solomon was never dressed so fine.

15 Man hath still either toys or care,
    He hath no root, nor to one place is tied,
    But ever restless and irregular
     About this Earth doth run and ride;
    He knows he hath a home, but scarce knows where;
20   He says it is so far
    That he hath quite forgot how to go there.

    He knocks at all doors, strays and roams,
    Nay, hath not so much wit as some stones have,
    Which in the darkest nights point to their homes
25 By some hid sense their Maker gave;
    Man is the shuttle, to whose winding quest
             And passage through these looms
    God ordered motion, but ordained no rest.

Cock-crowing

     Father of lights! what sunny seed,
     What glance of day hast thou confined
     Into this bird? To all the breed
     This busy ray thou hast assigned;
5   Their magnetism works all night,
      And dreams of Paradise and light.

12   *tinned* – kindled, or made shine, like new tin.

13   *tincture* – essence: an alchemaic term.

17–18   *If a mere blast ... prevail* – the idea here draws on the second part of the quotation from *Anima Magica Abscondita* (see page 186).

20–22   *Whose hand ... the same* – the workings of the Lord are visible through and by everything that He created.

29   *dark, Egyptian border* – Exodus 10.21: 'And the Lord said unto Moses, Stretch out thine hand toward heaven, that there may be darkness over the land of Egypt, even darkness which may be felt.'

37   *veil which thou has broke* – II Corinthians 2.14: '...until this day remaineth the same veil untaken away in the reading of the old testament: which veil is done away in Christ.'

Their eyes watch for the morning hue,
Their little grain expelling night
So shines and sings, as if it knew
10 The path unto the house of light.
 It seems their candle, howe'er done,
 Was tinned and lighted at the sun.

If such a tincture, such a touch,
So firm a longing can impower
15 Shall thy own image think it much
To watch for thy appearing hour?
 If a mere blast so fill the sail,
 Shall not the breath of God prevail?

Oh thou immortal light and heat!
20 Whose hand so shines through all this frame,
That by the beauty of the seat,
We plainly see, who made the same,
 Seeing thy seed abides in me,
 Dwell thou in it, and I in thee.

25 To sleep without thee, is to die;
Yea, 'tis a death partakes of hell:
For where thou dost not close the eye
It never opens, I can tell.
 In such a dark, Egyptian border,
30 The shades of death dwell and disorder.

If joys, and hopes, and earnest throes,
And hearts, whose pulse beats still for light
Are given to birds; who, but thee, knows
A love-sick soul's exalted flight?
35 Can souls be tracked by any eye
 But his, who gave them wings to fly?

Only this veil which thou hast broke,
And must be broken yet in me,

48   *lily* – the lily is the flower of light.

The Night

John 3.2: '(Nicodemus) came to Jesus by night, and said until him, Rabbi, we
know that thou are a teacher come from God: for no man can do these
miracles that thou doest, except God be with him.'

This is one of Vaughan's most mystic poems, which works on the paradox
of night revealing the true nature of God, which is concealed from man in the
distractions of day-time. Superficially, this may appear to contradict
Vaughan's ideas expressed in such poems as The *Morning-watch* or *Cock-
crowing*. It should be read, however, as an alternative mystical exploration of
ideas about the revelation and nature of God, seen through images drawn
from the natural world.

*Setting aside the ideas expressed in this poem, how do you respond to it as a
description of night?*

1–2   *Virgin-shrine* ... *sacred veil* – the fleshly body of Christ, derived from
         the Virgin Mary, which conceals and reveals His divinity.

   3   *glow-worms* – insects which emit light at night as a mating device,
         thought to look always towards the moon and to reflect its glow.

   5   *Nicodemus* – in John 3, Nicodemus is identified as a Pharisee and
         ruler of the Jews, asking questions of Jesus which elicit answers
         about the rebirth of the spirit.

   9   *healing wings* – Malachi 4.2: '...shall the Sun of righteousness arise
         with healing in his wings'.

  14   *He* – i.e. Nicodemus.

This veil, I say, is all the cloak
40 And cloud which shadows thee from me.
    This veil thy full-eyed love denies,
    And only gleams and fractions spies.

    O take it off! make no delay,
    But brush me with thy light, that I
45 May shine upon a perfect day,
    And warm me at thy glorious Eye!
        O take it off! or till it flee,
        Though with no lily, stay with me!

The Night

    Through that pure Virgin-shrine,
    That sacred veil drawn o'er thy glorious noon,
    That men might look and live, as glow-worms shine,
        And face the moon,
5   Wise Nicodemus saw such light
    As made him know his God by night.

    Most blest believer he!
    Who in that land of darkness and blind eyes
    Thy long-expected healing wings could see,
10   When thou didst rise,
    And, what can never more be done,
    Did at midnight speak with the Sun!

    Oh who will tell me where
    He found thee at that dead and silent hour!
15 What hollowed solitary ground did bear
            So rare a flower,
        Within whose sacred leaves did lie
        The fulness of the Deity?

19–20 *mercy-seat of gold … cherub* – Exodus 25: 'And thou shalt make a
mercy-seat of pure gold … and thou shalt make two cherubims of
gold …'

29 *Christ's progress* – two passages in the New Testament refer to
Christ rising before dawn to pray in the open air.

32–3 *When my Lord's head … drops of night* – Song of Solomon 5.2: 'I
sleep, but my heart waketh: it is the voice of my beloved that
knocketh, saying, Open to me, my sister, my love, my dove, my
undefiled: for my head is filled with dew, and my locks with the
drops of the night.'

No mercy-seat of gold,
20 No dead and dusty cherub, nor carved stone,
But his own living works did my Lord hold
              And lodge alone;
      Where trees and herbs did watch and peep
      And wonder, while the Jews did sleep.

25   Dear night! this world's defeat;
The stop to busy fools; care's check and curb;
The day of spirits; my soul's calm retreat
              Which none disturb!
      Christ's progress, and his prayer time;
30   The hours to which high Heaven doth chime;

      God's silent, searching flight;
When my Lord's head is filled with dew, and all
His locks are wet with the clear drops of night;
              His still, soft call;
35   His knocking time; the soul's dumb watch,
      When spirits their fair kindred catch.

      Were all my loud, evil days
Calm and unhaunted as is thy dark tent,
Whose peace but by some angel's wing or voice
40   Is seldom rent,
      Then I in Heaven all the long year
      Would keep, and never wander here.

      But living where the sun
Doth all things wake, and where all mix and tire
45 Themselves and others, I consent and run
              To every mire,
      And by this world's ill-guiding light,
      Err more than I can do by night.

50 *A deep, but dazzling darkness* – Vaughan draws on a concept
    expounded by a fifth/sixth-century writer, known as Dionysius the
    Areopagite, who influenced later generations of mystic writers. As
    the Creator, God contains the essence of all things, which are seen
    imperfectly by man. Darkness, in its purest form, is revelatory: on
    earth it conceals, but in heaven it reveals.

The Waterfall

This is a direct use of an aspect of nature to provide an extended conceit
which explores Vaughan's spiritual longings. To an extent, it can be regarded
as an emblematic poem, with the first verse paragraph mirroring the
wandering stream, the second the straight fall of the waterfall itself.

How does reading this poem aloud increase understanding?

There is in God (some say)
50 A deep, but dazzling darkness; as men here
Say it is late and dusky, because they
See not all clear.
Oh for that night! where I in him
Might live invisible and dim.

The Waterfall

With what deep murmurs through time's silent stealth
Doth thy transparent, cool and wat'ry wealth
Here flowing fall,
And chide, and call,
5 As if his liquid, loose retinue staid
Ling'ring, and were of this steep place afraid,
The common pass
Where, clear as glass,
All must descend
10 Not to an end:
But quick'ned by this deep and rocky grave,
Rise to a longer course more bright and brave.

Dear stream! dear bank, where often I
Have sat, and pleased my pensive eye,
15 Why, since each drop of thy quick store
Runs thither, whence it flowed before,
Should poor souls fear a shade or night,
Who came (sure) from a sea of light?
Or since those drops are all sent back
20 So sure to thee, that none doth lack,
Why should frail flesh doubt any more
That what God takes, he'll not restore?
O useful element and clear!
My sacred wash and cleanser here,
25 My first consigner unto those

26 *Fountains ... goes* – Revelation 7.17: 'For the Lamb ... shall lead them unto living fountains of waters.'

30–31 *... that Spirit ... move* – Genesis 1.2: 'And the Spirit of God moved upon the face of the waters.'

38 *My glorious liberty* – Romans 8.21: '... the glorious liberty of the children of God.'

Fountains of life, where the Lamb goes!
What sublime truths and wholesome themes
Lodge in thy mystical, deep streams!
Such as dull man can never find
30   Unless that Spirit lead his mind
Which first upon thy face did move,
And hatched all with his quick'ning love.
As this loud brook's incessant fall
In streaming rings restagnates all,
35   Which reach by course the bank, and then
Are no more seen, just so pass men.
O my invisible estate,
My glorious liberty, still late!
Thou art the channel my soul seeks,
40   Not this with cataracts and creeks.

CHRONOLOGICAL TABLE

Date	Events in poets' lives	Other events
1572	Birth of Donne	
1577		Drake circumnavigates world
1588		Defeat of Spanish Armada
1593	Birth of Herbert	
1594	Birth of Carew	
1596/7	Donne on Essex expeditions	
1600		Essex rebellion
1601	Donne's marriage to Ann More	
1603		Death of Elizabeth I, accession of James I
1605		Gunpowder Plot
1609	Herbert at Trinity, Cambridge Birth of Crashaw	/10 Publication of works by Kepler and Galileo proving earth moves round the sun
1611		Publication of King James Bible (Authorized Version)
1612	Carew graduates from Merton	
1615	Donne ordained	
1616	Herbert elected Fellow of Trinity	Death of Shakespeare
1621	Donne appointed Dean of St Paul's Birth of Marvell and Vaughan	
1623		Publication of Shakespeare First Folio
1624	Herbert ordained	
1625		Death of James I, accession of Charles I
1629		Dissolution of Parliament
1630	Carew appointed Gentleman of the Privy Chamber Herbert appointed Vicar of Bemerton	
1631	Death of Donne	
1633	First edition of Donne's *Songs and Sonnets*, including Carew's *Elegy* Death of Herbert: posthumous publication of *The Temple*	
1635	Crashaw appointed Fellow of Peterhouse	

Date	Events in poets' lives	Other events
1638	Vaughan at Jesus College, Oxford (?)	
1639	Marvell graduates from Trinity	
1640	Death of Carew	Short Parliament
		Long Parliament (–1653)
1642		Civil War
1645	Crashaw in Rome	New Model Army
1646	Crashaw publishes *Steps to the Temple*	End of first Civil War
1648	Death of Vaughan's brother William	Second Civil War
1649	Death of Crashaw	Execution of Charles I
		Abolition of monarchy
		Commonwealth declared
1650	Vaughan publishes first volume of *Silex Scintillans*	
	Marvel tutor to Mary Fairfax	
1652	Posthumous publication of Crashaw's *Carmen Deo Nostro*	
1653	Marvell tutor to William Dutton, Cromwell's ward	Cromwell Lord Protector
1655	Vaughan publishes second volume of *Silex Scintillans*	War with Spain
1657	Marvell appointed Latin Secretary to Council of State	
1659	Marvell MP for Hull	Rump Parliament
1660		Restoration of monarchy
		Accession of Charles II
1665		War with Holland
		Plague
1666		Great Fire of London
1678	Death of Marvell	
1685		Death of Charles II
		Accession of James II
		Monmouth Rebellion
1689		Accession of William and Mary
1695	Death of Vaughan	

CRITICAL APPROACHES

The following commentary concentrates on placing metaphysical poetry in the context of its time, and attempts to suggest ways in which a modern-day reader can approach it. It concludes with a brief section which highlights technical aspects of this poetry, and explains some of the critical terminology which is often associated with it.

Metaphysical poetry: a historical perspective

The poets whose work appears in this edition did not call themselves 'metaphysicals'. The label was attached to them in the eighteenth century, with Dryden, Pope and Johnson using the term when writing about a style of poetry which was, by then, thought to be obscure, difficult and generally unappealing. Another label which at times has been applied is the 'School of Donne'. Undoubtedly, John Donne was of great influence on many fellow- and succeeding poets, but he never set out to teach others how to write this kind of poetry. Rather, his writing appeared at a particular moment in time, and his style and subject-matter synthesized and gave a clear voice to ideas which characterized certain aspects of the age in which he lived. Subsequent writers employed similar approaches, each adapting the style to their particular needs, and speaking with their own voices.

Fashion in literature is like any other trend; a style emerges which seems to express what is exciting, relevant, adoptable. It flourishes, develops, is adapted and renewed by its followers up to a certain point. Then it is overtaken by another, which in turn becomes the voice of its age. This is what happened to metaphysical poetry. If one looks at what went before it, one can see the seeds of the style in the irregular and distinctive verse of Thomas Wyatt, who was writing in the reign of Henry VIII, in some of the lyrical poetry of the early and mid-Elizabethan period and, in particular, in the compression and discipline of the sonnet form, both Petrarchan and Shakespearean. Later writers, such as Marvell, are as clearly of their own age as Donne is of his, but the legacy of Donne's literary approach is still obvious.

The lives of those who have become termed 'metaphysical' poets spanned a century, from the age of Elizabeth I to that of James II. However, the turn of the seventeenth century into the eighteenth century saw inevitable changes in literary attitudes and styles, following the political and social upheavals of the previous century. It is interesting that it was a poet, Dryden, who appears to have been one of the first to use the term disparagingly, when writing of Donne:

'He affects the metaphysics, not only in his satires, but in his amorous verses, where nature only should reign; and perplexes the minds of the fair sex with nice speculations of philosophy . . .' (1693)

Thereafter, until the twentieth century, the style of poetry known as metaphysical seemed to have had little appeal, either to scholars or to the reading public. It was considered difficult, over-demanding, some of it harsh and unmellifluous. Succeeding ages established new criteria for critical and popular responses to poetry, and judged that what they valued as beautiful in poetic form was sacrificed, by the metaphysical poets, to the demands of argument. Wit, in the way in which these poets used it, was generally suspect, as were their attitudes to sacred and profane love – religion and sex.

The twentieth century has seen a change in this attitude. Influential writers, in particular the poet T.S. Eliot, and scholars such as Grierson and Gardner, provided re-evaluation which stripped away intervening assumptions about the 'true' nature of poetry, and allowed their contemporaries, and their successors, to make independent and uncluttered judgements. Critical writing during the twentieth century has done much to demystify the term 'metaphysical'. It is now mainly recognized and used as a convenient designation for a number of seventeenth-century poets whose writing exhibits, to varying degrees, a fusion of thought and feeling, in which the intellect is a powerful crafting instrument, and in which experiences and ideas are explored and presented with vigour and originality. The voices of these poets now speak directly to readers living many centuries later, and, for many, they speak in ways and say things which are understandable. Though they lived so long ago, we seem to have much in common with them. Basic human experience is unchanging; the variations created by the immediate circumstances of the age are, perhaps, less marked than may be superficially apparent. These poets may present us with challenges, but we are equipped to meet them.

Metaphysical poetry and the spirit of the age

When reading the work of any writer, any poet, it is essential to recognize the cultural signposts which place a work in the context of its time and the preoccupations of that time. Thus, an understanding of Thomas Hardy's poem *The Darkling Thrush* is dependent on noting its date of composition, 31st December 1900. Hardy's focus was precise, and the metaphorical content of the poem is determined by its own moment in time. This is not to suggest any greater similarity between the writings of Hardy and these earlier poets, it is simply to illustrate the fact that the poet's craft does not operate in a vacuum, and appreciation of context allows us to read from an informed perspective. Coming closer to the present time, a poem such as Tony Harrison's *"V"*, which takes as its impetus the desecration of the poet's parents' grave with graffiti, and moves on to examine with tough sensitivity and complete poetic control fundamental aspects of human nature and the society which generated such an act, contains symbols and references which speak directly to late twentieth-century readers, but may need to be explained to readers living a few centuries further into the future.

If we look at Donne, we see a poet who was writing at the turn of a century. As the sixteenth century changes into the seventeenth, his poetry seems to exemplify the sense of instability, uncertainty, yet excitement which this moment in time embodies. Marvell, writing fifty years later, lived through civil war, saw the deposition and execution of one king, the restoration of another. In the last years of the twentieth century, and the early years of the twenty-first, what experiences and emotions do we share with those who lived so long before us? Is our world so very different from theirs? Our age is post-Holocaust, post-Hiroshima; poverty, war, famine, disease, religious and racial persecution, are still endemic to humanity. Man has stood on the moon, sent space vessels to distant planets, yet the tensions between ideologies and nations, fears of ecological disaster, the growing gap between rich and poor, all ensure that our times are as uncertain and unstable as any seen as such from a historical perspective. Yet, at the same time, mankind's inventiveness, both scientific and artistic, continues to create excitement and stimulation, and is, perhaps, shared by more people than ever before. Are there parallels between our times, and those of these poets?

The spirit of the age of the poets whose work appears in this collection was one of change, danger, social and political upheaval. It was one of artistic richness, of barbarism and of sensitivity. The plays of Shakespeare were performed alongside a bear-baiting pit; a poet could pen a sonnet to his mistress before attending a public execution, seeing the victim disembowelled whilst still alive. There were great discoveries, and great uncertainties. The voyages of exploration of the fifteenth century had opened new continents to explorers and adventurers; the astrological investigations of Galileo and Copernicus had overturned the ordered, geocentric, medieval model of the universe, providing poets with an even wider range of sources of imagery.

Established religious doctrines were challenged. Since the Anglican secession from Rome in the reign of Henry VIII, there had been many changes to what was acceptable as personal faith. Protestants and Catholics died in turn for their faith, and the sterner doctrines of Calvinism and Puritanism were gaining ground. Traditional beliefs in the nature of kingship, the ways in which society was ordered, were questioned. The Essex rebellion against Elizabeth, the Gunpowder Plot against James I, both indicated a basically unstable monarchy, culminating in the challenge to what was thought to be the divine right of kings, the Civil War and the execution of Charles I. The establishment of the Commonwealth under Cromwell did not provide unity and harmony, and the restoration of the monarchy provided only intermittent periods of calm.

Reading and responding

The Modern Perspective

If there are problems for readers nowadays in responding to the metaphysical poets, where do they lie? Is the attitude to religion a stumbling-block? Our age has seen a rise in religious fundamentalism throughout the world, and we can witness, if we do not experience, the power that religion holds over human emotions and behaviour. The intensity of personal religious experience is, perhaps, less apparent. Belief in heaven and hell, eternal bliss or everlasting torment, seems to have waned in all save a few. Equally, does it matter that the sexual relationships which these poets write about are male-dominated, even though the power of the mistress is poetically acknowledged? Society was, then, ordered thus, and these poets wrote in that context. (Women were composing poetry, and plays, in the seventeenth century. Mary Wroth, Katherine Philips and Margaret Cavendish were known poets, and Aphra Behn was a successful playwright. However, a discussion of their work is beyond the scope of this edition.) If, as readers, we look beyond the surface – the argument, or the occasion of a poem – to the emotion which is its generative force, we can begin to share common experience with these writers, and to respond empathically, but with some critical objectivity, to what they wrote.

Poet as Writer and Subject

A basic question to be asked of a poet and his poems is, who is the speaker? This is a question which often has to remain open, affording interesting speculation rather than a neat explanation. It is not possible to say, with certainty, that in the case of a certain poet the narrating 'I' who appears in the poems is always the poet, presenting himself without disguise. The self-dramatization with which Donne recreates and presents the immediacy of real or imagined situations may encourage his readers to believe that he is presenting himself to us, in some cases naked and unashamed. But we cannot be certain.

It has already been noted that Donne (and Herbert) lived in a great age of theatre, and vivid dramatization, and the power of dialogue, were an important aspect of their cultural context. Both these poets' voices are unmistakably individual, as is that of Vaughan, another poet who places himself as an active participant in the drama of religious enquiry. The religious poetry of these three poets reveals much about their characters; their poems are stages on a path of continuing self-questioning and re-affirmation of faith, and we feel that we begin to know the man behind the poem. Equally, there is a consistency of voice in some of Donne's love poems which encourages the reader to feel that the poet who appears in such poems, and the poet who wrote them, are very much the same person. However, it would be wrong to assume that poems in which the poet appears to conceal himself, either by non-appearance or by possible assumption of a fictional persona, are insincere, either in divine or secular poetry. Marvell can present himself as a detached observer or as a bemused participant (as in *The Garden*). He seems, perhaps more than the other poets in this volume, to have hidden himself deliberately, and with skill, but, throughout the range of his poetry, there is an individual voice which places a unique signature on his work.

Crashaw addresses, elaborates on and embellishes his subjects in a style which is unmistakably different from that of Marvell, whilst Carew's poetry shows, perhaps, more craftsmanship than emotion, though his *Elegy* for Donne seems to have been inspired by true respect, and to demonstrate informed understanding of that writer's techniques and achievement.

Love and Death, Religion and Sex – and the Power of Reason

Timor mortis conturbat me (the fear of death perturbs me). This is the refrain of a poem written by William Dunbar, a Scottish poet and priest, late in the fifteenth century, and it states succinctly a basic truth. He, and these poets who came later, wrote in times when religious belief was universal, and the fear of something after death was real and ever-present. The only possibility of salvation was through the redemption of Christ. This statement is a gross simplification of the complexities presented by the different religious doctrines (Catholic and Protestant, Calvinist, Puritan and High Anglican) which continued to struggle for supremacy, but there were very few, whatever their allegiance, who lived without that fear.

Terror of what might happen after death is rarely stated more vividly than in Shakespeare's *Measure for Measure*, Claudio's speech in Act III scene i: 'Ay, but to die, and go we know not where . . .', and the ever-present certainty of death in a turbulent age provoked intense responses. On the one side lay the pursuit and enjoyment of sexual pleasure which, at its best, was based on a real and sustained loving relationship. This provided some reassurance and consolation, a kind of defiance of the inevitable. It is not for nothing that the word 'die' acquired its second meaning, to achieve orgasm. But this secular love was, in many ways, a substitute, or a diversion. Love of God, usually through Christ, whose human form provided a recognizable focus for devotion, was the true purpose of mankind. Redemption could only be achieved because Christ expressed his love for mankind through willing and positive self-sacrifice, the Crucifixion.

Thus, religious love is as passionate as secular love, and is conveyed with equal force. In the twelfth century, an anonymous cleric wrote a treatise for anchorites (enclosed nuns). Much of it is in allegorical terms, presenting Christ as lover, and in it He is made to say: 'I desire you to be either entirely cold, or entirely hot, in love of me; for if you are equal between the two, neither hot nor cold, you will disgust me, and I will spew you out . . .' (rendered in modern English). This avoidance of tepidity in love, particularly religious love, can be seen in the work of these poets, five centuries later, from Donne's self-analytical challenge, through Herbert's joyous yet grave courtesy, Vaughan's mysticism, to Crashaw's erotic imagery, which seems to look straight back at his medieval predecessor.

The one thing that the poet could depend on, as it was God-given, was the power of reason. It is reason which raises man above the lower orders of creation, and links him to the higher. Through reason, he can compose and develop argument; his intelligence (wit) enables him to shape and re-present his questioning, his demands, his understanding. Thus he has at least a limited power over his immediate destiny. Applied to sexual love, this power of reason may persuade a willing mistress to grant temporary respite from anxiety through the little death, sexual satisfaction. When used in the service of religion, it may ameliorate the pangs of the greater death, through argument which convinces the poet to believe and to repent, and thus achieve redemption.

The language of analysis

When writing about literature, of any kind, it is essential to be able to use a vocabulary which describes accurately, in terms which are generally understood and accepted, what you wish to say about a writer's crafting of material. Much of the critical vocabulary which is in general use is as applicable to metaphysical poetry as it is to any other kind of writing. It is not necessary to find different terms for (for example) *metre, rhyme, rhythm, verse structure, syntax, alliteration, assonance*. Equally, the words which can be used to describe the effect which a writer has achieved, which describe mood and tone, the development of argument, the opening and conclusion of a poem, can all be drawn from the wider lexicon.

Familiarity with and use of analytical language empowers a student to pursue exploration and discussion, and make an informed personal response. However, this is supplemental to the direct engagement with the text, and the close reading, consideration and thought which are essential to serious and enjoyable study. It is never enough to learn a check-list of critical terms, and then apply them mechanically within whatever task is given. They should be used as an aid to demonstrate understanding, not replace it.

There are, however, a number of terms which are used in discussion of metaphysical poetry, which, though not exclusive to it, are generally accepted and understood as accurate descriptors of aspects of writing which are particular to these poets. Some of this terminology has been used, where appropriate, in notes and commentary within this edition. The following brief list aims to define and explain such terms.

strong line This term is, perhaps, not used nowadays as frequently as it once was, but it is a useful one to describe a particular feature of much metaphysical poetry. Originally used with reference to prose as well as poetry, it refers to the compression and succinctness of expression, producing a density of ideas and meaning, which demands the reader's concentrated and alert attention. This tight discipline, of both writer and reader, was thought by some commentators to result in poetry which was self-indulgently difficult, and harsh in expression. Those who admire the intellectual rigour, precision and flair of such writing may well use it as a term of approbation.

elliptical syntax This refers to sentences in which some words which would be required for complete clarity are omitted. It is a feature of *strong lines.*

paradox This term has wide and general use, but it is one which describes something which is a regular feature of metaphysical poetry. The dictionary definition is 'a seemingly absurd or contradictory statement', and the key word here is 'seemingly'; the paradox can reveal unexpected truths, proving that apparent contradictions are, in fact, statements whose meanings are collectively and severally equally valid.

wit The modern use of this word, which defines it almost exclusively as 'humour', distorts its meaning and application to the crafting of poetry. A more appropriate definition for this purpose is 'directing intelligence', the ability to re-define, to draw together apparently conflicting ideas, to pursue and present argument and ideas in a fresh and enlightening way, which gives satisfaction to the writer in the exercise of creativity, and pleasure to the reader in its result.

conceit   This is the one term which is most used by commentators on metaphysical poetry. Dr Johnson, in the eighteenth century, described it as 'a combination of dissimilar images, or discovery of occult resemblances in things apparently unalike'. This is probably as useful a definition as can be found; subsequent commentators have expanded upon it, but generally the idea of 'unlikely likeness' lies at the heart of discussion of the conceit. The word 'occult' in Johnson's definition seems particularly apt when speaking of metaphysical poetry, as he was using it in the sense of esoteric, mysterious, beyond everyday knowledge, all of which terms can well be applied to many features of this poetry.

The conceit demands that the reader concedes its appropriateness to that point of discourse or argument which it sustains, whilst recognizing that it is a new-coined, startling, original concept. Things chosen to create the conceit usually bear little or no apparent likeness to the things to which it is applied. The conceit differs from simile and metaphor. Both of those may encourage the reader's (and the poet's) mind to wander and speculate about supposed resemblances, or the resonances inherent within the images which are created. The embellishing quality of such techniques distracts from the rigour of argument which the conceit is designed to support and sustain, and bring to a satisfactory conclusion.

EXPLORATION AND DISCUSSION

The following section suggests approaches to study of individual poems and groups of poems. These suggestions are provided as starting-points and signposts for close reading and detailed discussion. Many of the approaches can be applied across the whole area of study, whilst some are more closely focused on particular poems. They can be used as a stimulus, and students should select those which they find most interesting and useful to their individual studies.

John Donne

Elegies

To his Mistress Going to Bed and *On his Mistress*

1   In both these elegies, Donne is addressing his mistress directly. In *To his Mistress Going to Bed*, is he inviting, or commanding? How does the tone compare with that of *On his Mistress*?

2   Note the different kinds of images which Donne draws on in *To his Mistress Going to Bed*. How are they used for the purpose of persuasion? How effective are they in conveying to the reader the progress of the experience which he is describing?

3   Analyse the syntax of the first twelve lines of *On his Mistress*. Why do you think that Donne delays his two exhortations ('I calmly beg' and 'Thou shalt not love . . .')? How does the structure of this first sentence in the poem relate to the main theme?

4   In *On his Mistress*, identify the various reasons why Donne does not wish his mistress to elope with him.

5   Look at lines 51–4 of *On his Mistress*. How do they differ from the rest of the poem, and what do you find of interest about them?

6   In line 4 of *On his Mistress* Donne write of his 'words' masculine persuasive force', and in line 30 of his mistress's 'womanly discovering

grace'. How do these concepts relate to the rest of this poem, and to Donne's writing in general?

7   Which of these two poems do you prefer, and why?

Songs and Sonnets

The Flea

1   How is the argument constructed in this poem? Note what is described in each stanza, and how this is used as stages in the argument. How does Donne create a satisfactory conclusion in the last three lines?

2   What is the effect of the combination of religious and sexual imagery?

3   Discuss the relative importance of the 'three' (flea, mistress, poet) in terms of their relationship within the wooing process which the poem undertakes.

The Good Morrow

1   How do the lines 1–4 of the first stanza differ from the rest of the poem? Why do you think they are written in this way? How does the poem take a new direction after this, and what new ideas are introduced?

2   What is the effect of the repeated 'Let' in the second stanza?

3   Note the images which Donne uses in this poem. Where else can similar images be found in his poetry? Compare the way in which he uses them here with their use in other poems.

4   Consider the different ways in which the final couplet can be read. How do the variations affect your reading and understanding of the whole poem?

5   What is Donne saying about love in this poem?

Song (Go, and catch . . .)

1   What is the cumulative effect of the 'strange sights' which Donne presents in the first stanza? How does Donne build on these in the second stanza to create a sense of the fabulous?

2 How would you describe the tone of the final stanza?

3 Analyse the form of this poem. How does it suit the ideas which Donne is presenting?

The Undertaking

In this poem, Donne constructs an argument about the nature of true love, and comments on how it may be perceived and misinterpreted by others. Does the form which Donne chooses here help to clarify it? What is the importance of the opening and closing stanzas in the handling of the argument?

The Sun Rising

1 The sun is a frequent source of subject-matter and imagery for poets, and Donne used it many times, both in his love poetry and his divine poems, sometimes punningly. What is unique about the way in which the sun is written about here? Reference to *The Oxford Book of Quotations* will give some material for comparison.

2 Trace the visual line throughout the poem. How does the poet's physical gaze shift, and how is the reader aware of this?

3 In the first stanza, Donne presents a series of pairings and lists. What is their effect? How do the images in the second stanza differ from those in the first, and why?

4 Comment on the impact of the first two lines of the third stanza. How do you react to them? How would you describe the tone of the closing of the poem? Does it differ from the opening? If so, in what way?

5 How important do you think it is to read this (and many of Donne's poems) with an awareness of the contemporary culture, and of the ways in which relationships between men and women were understood at the time the poem was written?

6 Why do you think this is one of the most frequently anthologized of Donne's poems?

The Canonization

1 Discuss who do you think this poem is addressed to.

2 Identify the subjects which provide the conceits in stanzas two, three and four. How does the imagery change as the argument progresses?

3 How does Donne resolve the argument in the final stanza?

4 What do you think is meant by the title of this poem?

Song (Sweetest love . . .)

1 Compare this poem with *On his Mistress* and *A Valediction: forbidding Mourning*, as a poem which deals with the parting of lovers. What differences, and what similarities, can you find in tone and subject-matter? How do the different verse forms used for these poems affect your reading of them?

2 Which of the three poems appeals to you most, and why?

Air and Angels

1 How well do you think this poem expresses the experience of being in love?

2 Which phrases and lines from this poem do you find most memorable, and why?

The Anniversary

1 Identify the ideas which this poem shares with *The Sun Rising*. What differences are there in the way in which Donne uses them here?

2 Donne introduces the concept of the passage of time in the first stanza. How does he do so, and for what purpose? How does he use it at the end of the poem?

3 How does the second stanza provide a transition in thought between the opening and closing of the poem?

4 What is the tone of the poem? How is it achieved? Is it consistent throughout the poem, or can you detect any changes?

Twickenham Garden

1 The best way to become aware of the rhythms of a poem is to read it aloud. Try reading this poem aloud with a partner, and mark where you feel the words should be stressed. Are there similar patterns in each

stanza? How do they vary? How do rhythms in the different stanzas help to convey the mood which Donne is creating in this poem?

2   How do you respond to Donne's use of the doctrine of transubstantiation, and the Biblical references, in the first stanza?

3   Does the conventional excuse (frustrated love) which is offered for the poet's anguish weaken, or clarify, the mood of despair?

A Valediction: of Weeping

1   How do the structure of the stanzas, and the rhyme scheme, suit Donne's purpose?

2   Note how the things which Donne chooses as images change in size, texture and substance. Do they have any constant features?

3   Trace the development of argument and how it relates to the conceits which are central to each stanza.

4   Why you think Donne changes the dominant element from water to wind in the closing lines?

A Nocturnal upon St Lucy's Day

1   What similarities, and what differences, in mood and content can you find between this poem and *Twickenham Garden*?

2   What is the effect of the recurrent alliteration on 's' throughout the poem?

3   How do you respond to the fourth stanza, and the idea that the poet does not wish to be an 'ordinary nothing'? What is the subsequent impact of the opening of the last stanza?

4   Attempt to identify and define the mood of this poem. Test your theories by reading it aloud. Go on to find ways of writing about what you have discovered, referring to the language, structure, rhythms and rhyme of the poem, stating how all these combine to produce a particular effect. Remember that these are your own thoughts, and that there is not a 'right' answer: if you can justify your own ideas by a close analysis which is sensitive to the way in which Donne has crafted his ideas, that is a valid response.

A Valediction: forbidding Mourning

1 How do the images of the opening stanza relate to the ideas explored in the rest of the poem?

2 The poem is written in simple, regular quatrains. Compare the way in which Donne uses this form here with the way he does so in other poems. Is the poem metrically regular? Where do irregularities occur, and what is their effect?

3 Explore the conceits which Donne uses throughout the poem. How do they relate to each other, and how does he use them to further his argument? How does his use of conceits here compare with (say) those in *A Valediction: of Weeping*?

4 Why do you think that the 'compass' conceit is so often mentioned by commentators on Donne's poems? Do you think that it does exemplify an aspect of Donne's writing?

The Funeral and The Relic

1 Explore the different ways in which Donne uses the central motif of the 'bracelet of bright hair about the bone'.

2 What other ideas do the poems have in common? In what ways do they differ?

3 How does the final stanza of *The Relic* contrast with the rest of the poem?

The Prohibition

1 Examine the effect of the opening and closing lines of each stanza.

2 Explore the ways in which Donne balances, and builds on, the themes of love and hate throughout the poem, and note the images associated with these concepts.

3 Trace the development of the argument through the poem. Is its resolution logical?

The Expiration

1 To gain some idea of what such a poem might sound like when set to music, try to find a recording of the music for voice of a composer of the

late sixteenth/early seventeenth century, such as Campion, Johnson or Gibbons. The melodic structure and the way in which the words are used are very different from later classical music.

2 How does Donne use the long 'o' sound in this poem, and how does he combine it with different kinds of pauses, particularly when used in a monosyllable?

Holy Sonnets

This is my play's . . .

1 Note the series of conceits in the first four lines. Why do you think Donne chose these images as the opening, and how do they relate to the rest of the sonnet?

2 Comment on 'gluttonous death'. What visual image does it offer? How does it compare with the way in which Donne writes about death elsewhere in the *Holy Sonnets*?

3 How appropriate do you find the final line as a conclusion to the argument of the poem?

At the round earth's . . .

1 Is there a shift in tone between the octave and sestet of this sonnet? If so, for what reason, and how is it achieved?

2 What is the effect of the enjambment of the first four lines, and of the long list in lines 6 and 7?

Death be not proud . . .

1 How does this sonnet differ in ideas and content from the other *Holy Sonnets* printed here?

2 Describe Donne's attitude to death as it appears here. Can you find similar attitudes to other subjects elsewhere in Donne's poems? How does his approach here compare with those?

3 How do you respond to the final half-line of the poem?

What if this present . . .

1 Some commentators have found the shift in subject-matter between

the image of the crucified Christ, in the octave, and Donne's 'profane mistresses', in the sestet, remarkable, even shocking. How do you respond to it?

2 To what extent does the opening line of the poem prepare you for what follows?

Batter my heart . . .

1 How would you describe the tone of this sonnet? How has this been created?

2 Discuss the use of lists here, and make a comparison with the ways in which Donne uses them in other poems.

3 Explore the imagery of the sestet. How do you respond to the way in which Donne writes here about his relationship with God? What is the effect of the paradoxes in the final lines?

I am a little world . . .

1 Compare the ways in which Donne uses similar conceits here and in A Valediction: of Weeping.

2 What is the effect of the exclamations in lines 4 and 10?

Since she whom I loved . . .

1 It has been suggested that this poem shows a remarkable lack of grief at the death of Donne's wife, and that she is dismissed early in the poem as irrelevant once Donne has established the ground for his argument. Is this your reading of the poem? Consider how you could argue against this contention.

Oh to vex me . . .

1 How does Donne use paradoxes and contradictions in this poem?

2 What is the tone here? From your readings of Donne's poetry in this collection, to what extent do you feel that this poem is characteristic of his writing?

Divine Poems

Good Friday, 1613. Riding Westward

1 How are spheres, souls, the sun, east and west used in the progress of the meditation?

2 Consider the appropriateness of rhyming couplets as the chosen poetic form here.

3 Remembering that Donne was not ordained a priest until 1615, and that this poem was composed two years earlier, what does it convey to you about the nature of Donne's religious feelings; and how?

A Hymn to God the Father

1 Identify the rhyme scheme used in this poem. Why do you think it was chosen, and how does it affect your reading?

2 Compare the syntax of the first two stanzas with that of the last. Why do you think it is changed?

3 How do you respond to the pun on 'done'? How important is it to the theme of the poem?

Further Activities

1 Identify the different kinds of poetic structure which Donne uses. Choosing examples of those which you find most interesting, describe them, and write your own ideas about why they were chosen, and their effect on the themes of the poems in which they were used.

2 Donne used many different techniques in his writing, including lists, repetition, alliteration and assonance, mid-line caesura. Choose poems in which you can identify examples of these techniques, and consider how they are used and to what effect.

3 Find a poem, (e.g. *A Valediction: forbidding Mourning*) in which the careful placing of polysyllabic words (such as 'trepidation', 'sublunary') balances shorter, mainly monosyllabic ones (such as 'spheres', 'love'). What do you find of interest in this technique?

4 Even in this limited selection of Donne's poetry, you will have noted

that there are many things which particularly interested him, as he repeatedly draws on them to supply material for argument. Make a list of those which you find most interesting and striking, and write a short paragraph, or a few sentences, on each, to describe their different uses.

5   What evidence can you find in Donne's poetry that he lived in an age of the theatre? of religious turmoil? of scientific discoveries? of exploration and colonization?

6   How would you write about Donne's openings and conclusions?

7   Discuss the similarities, and the differences, which you have discovered between Donne's love poetry and his religious poetry.

8   After you have read some of the love poetry and the religious poetry written by other poets in this selection, make your own comparisons between their writing and that of Donne, with the aim of identifying those aspects of approach, subject-matter and tone which characterize Donne's writing. (This should also enable you to draw similar conclusions about the other chosen poets.) You may find it useful to work with a partner on this activity, choosing together some poems to examine, then moving on to detailed individual exploration and a sharing and discussion of conclusions.

9   The poet Dryden, writing in 1693, said of Donne that he '. . . perplexes the minds of the fair sex with nice speculations of philosophy, when he should engage their hearts, and entertain them with the softness of love'. How do you respond to this charge?

10   Donne was a poet who was much admired by his contemporaries. Though most of his poetry was not published until after his death, much of it was circulated in manuscript, and he sent many of his poems to patrons and friends. When you have read the work of other poets in this collection, attempt to evaluate what it was about Donne's writing that other poets admired, and in what ways he may have influenced them. You may find Carew's *Elegy upon the Death of the Dean of Pauls, Dr John Donne* will assist you, but look for clues elsewhere in all the poems.

George Herbert

The Church-Floor and *The Windows*

1 Using material from these poems, write the opening paragraphs of a sermon which you feel Herbert might have preached.

2 Discuss the effect of the personifications used in the final stanza of *The Church-Floor*.

3 Trace the development of argument in both these poems.

Christmas, Good Friday and *Easter*

1 In all these poems, there is an abrupt change in the poetic structure at one point. Identify the structure used, and discuss the ways in which both halves of each poem are linked. Construct argument *for* and *against* the way in which *Good Friday* and *Easter* are printed in this edition, i.e. with the final stanzas as the completion of each poem, rather than separately.

2 Explore Herbert's use of the themes of beasts and man, light and darkness in *Christmas*.

3 Discuss the ways in which images of blood are used in *Good Friday*.

4 Trace the use of the extended conceit based on music in *Easter*. Note the way it is used in lines 11 and 12. What idea is Herbert presenting here? Explore your own reaction to these images.

5 What do you find song-like about the last parts of *Christmas* and *Easter*?

Jordan (I) and *(II)*, *Aaron*

1 Identify and note down examples of the kind of poetry Herbert refers to in stanza 2 of *Jordan (I)*. How do they compare with Herbert's poetry?

2 Trace the line of thematic development from *Jordan (I)* to *Jordan (II)*. Can you discern a difference in tone between the two poems? If so, how is it created?

3 Explore the ways in which ideas are linked to the Old and New Testaments in *Aaron*, and the ways in which Herbert uses them.

4 In *A Priest to The Temple*, Herbert wrote: 'The parson's . . apparel (is) plain, but reverend and clean, without spots, or dust, or smell; the purity of his mind breaking out and dilating itself even to his body, clothes, and habitation.' How are these ideas reflected in these three poems?

Prayer, The Pearl, Man, Life, Mortification, The Pulley, Death

1 In *Prayer*, Herbert builds the poem on a list of analogues for his subject. Explore the range of categories which he draws on, and identify the ways in which he achieves variety and interest.

2 Discuss the ways in which the title of *The Pearl*, and the quotation from which it derives, apply to the subject-matter of this poem.

3 How do you react to the idea that, in *Man*, Herbert presents concepts which are timeless, and as valid today as when the poem was written? Compare this poem with Vaughan's of the same title. What differences are there in attitude and approach?

4 Examine the images in *Life* which relate to the senses, and analyse the ways in which Herbert uses them.

5 Find and read some of the speeches in Shakespeare's plays which deal with man's life and its nature, to compare with Herbert's approach in *Mortification*. You could look at Jaques's speech in 2:i of *As You Like It*, the Duke's speech at the beginning of 3:i of *Measure for Measure*, and Hamlet's speeches in 5:i, the graveyard scene. What is characteristic about Herbert's writing on this theme?

6 Note the effect of the use of direct speech in *The Pulley*. What is the nature of God, as revealed in this poem? Why is the final gift reserved?

7 Explore your reactions to *Death*. Can it be described as a poem of comfort? If so, why and how? Read Donne's sonnet which begins: 'Death, be not proud . . .'. How does it compare, in tone and subject-matter, with this poem? What does the comparison tell you about the distinctive qualities of each poet?

Redemption, Affliction, Denial, The Collar, Love (III)

1 Explore the dramatic and narrative qualities of *Redemption*, and discuss why you feel Herbert chose the sonnet form to express his ideas in this poem.

2 Note the kinds of images Herbert uses in each stanza of *Affliction* to describe a different aspect of his life and experiences. How does the language he uses convey more than literal meaning?

3 Read *Denial* aloud, to help you to assess the particular quality of Herbert's handling of form and language in the service of the central idea. Discuss why you feel he repeats 'hearing' at the end of both the third and the fourth stanzas. Make a close analysis of the ways in which the final stanza differs from the former ones.

4 Some critics have suggested that *The Collar* is the most dramatic and passionate of Herbert's poems. From your reading of his writings, do you agree? You should consider the form and language of the poem as well as its ideas.

5 Explore your personal response to *Love (III)*. In what ways do you think its ideas, language and approach are characteristic of Herbert, from your study of his poems? Do you find it a fitting conclusion for a spiritual journey?

Further Activities

1 Evaluate the ways in which the ideas which Herbert himself expresses about the writing of poetry, and its purpose, are matched by the form and content of his own poems.

2 Identify and describe the verse forms used in these poems. Make your own notes about why and how Herbert used different forms for different subjects.

3 Choose a number of Herbert's poems which differ in tone from each other, and analyse the methods by which this has been achieved. Reading aloud will help you to gain initial impressions.

4 Make your own collection of the images used by Herbert which you find the most interesting, startling, pleasing or unpleasing. Analyse your reactions, and find ways of writing about them.

5 Explore the ways in which Herbert uses direct speech and dialogue, and their effect on the tone and argument of his poetry.

6 Discuss the dramatic qualities which you have found in Herbert's writing.

7 When you have read some of the poetry on religious themes written by other poets in this selection, discuss the ways in which Herbert's writing compares and contrasts with their works. You should aim to identify the particular qualities which Herbert's writing displays, and your personal response to them.

8 In *A Priest to The Temple*, Herbert wrote: 'The country parson is full of all knowledge. They say, it is an ill mason that refuseth any stone: and there is no knowledge, but, in a skilful hand, serves either positively as it is, or else to illustrate some other knowledge.' How can you apply this idea to Herbert's poetry?

9 Another quotation from *A Priest to The Temple*: 'The country parson preacheth constantly, the pulpit is his joy and his throne . . .' What impression of Herbert the preacher have you gained from his poetry?

Thomas Carew

Elegy upon the Death of the Dean of Paul's, Dr John Donne

1 Examine the series of questions which opens the poem. Why do you think Carew chose this approach?

2 Choose a section of the poem, of about 10–12 lines, and re-write it as continuous prose. Compare what you have written with the original. Have you had to add, or omit, any words or phrases? What changes have you made to the syntax? Have the changes made any difference to meaning? Has anything been lost, or gained, in the process? What conclusions about the nature of poetic expression can you draw from this exercise?

3 Examine where Carew places a strong mid-line caesura (pause). What effect does this have?

4 Read a section of the poem aloud. How aware are you of the rhyme scheme and metre in your reading? Note when and where Carew shifts the stress in a line. Why does he do this?

5 List the qualities which Carew admires in Donne's poetic achievement.

6 After you have studied Donne's poetry, discuss your feelings about Carew's estimation of his fellow-poet.

Mediocrity in Love Rejected

1 The concept of the mediocre, the middle way which makes no passionate commitment, is a theme which many writers have explored. Perhaps one of the most interesting (if rather inaccessible) is the late twelfth-century text *Ancrene Wisse* (a teaching for anchorites), in which tepid love for Christ is strongly attacked. Do you know of any other works, of any genre or time, which explore a similar theme?

2 Note how the diction used by Carew expresses the 'extreme' which he desires. List the words which carry this idea.

3 Examine Carew's use of contrasts, and the way in which he handles them to convey his theme.

To my inconstant Mistress

1 Read the poem aloud. Do the rhythms and rhyme scheme suggest a particular tone? What is it?

2 Note how Carew uses the language of religion in the poem. When he speaks of his 'strong faith', 'a fairer hand', and 'a soul more pure', do you think that he is referring to a human replacement for the 'inconstant mistress', or could he be speaking in straightforward religious terms? Do you think that the poem is deliberately ambiguous? Find ways of expressing your personal viewpoint on these questions.

Persuasions to enjoy

1 Read Marvell's *To his Coy Mistress*. What ideas and images do the two poems share?

2 Trace the alliteration on the letters 's' (and soft 'c'), 'f/v' and 'g', and consider its contribution to the lyrical qualities of the poem.

Boldness in Love

1 Examine the conceit in lines 7 and 8. What is Carew implying here? How effective is the conceit at this stage in the poem?

2 If you were to split this poem into two stanzas, where would you do so, and why?

Song

1 What is song-like about this poem?

2 Most of the words in this poem are monosyllabic. Note where Carew uses words of more than one syllable. Where does he place them? Is there a recognizable pattern? What is the effect of the longer words, where they are used?

3 What kind of images does Carew draw on in this poem, and how does he use them?

4 Sum up the idea which this poem explores in one succinct paragraph.

Further Activities

1 After you have studied both Donne's and Carew's poetry, evaluate the influence which you feel the older poet had on Carew. Go on to consider those aspects of Carew's writing which you think are individual to him, and where his creative strengths lie.

2 Define the areas which Carew drew on for his conceits. Under each heading, list your own choice of those you consider the most interesting, effective, or unexpected. Find a succinct and apt phrase or sentence to justify your choice in each case.

3 Explore the ways in which Carew matches poetic form to the themes of his poems.

4 Where and when do you detect a note of seriousness in Carew's poetry?

5 What do these poems have to say about Carew's attitude (and that of his contemporaries) to women and love-making?

Richard Crashaw

Hymn of the Nativity

1 Explore the way in which *the sun* is used in the first four stanzas. How

does this compare with the ways in which it is used by other metaphysical poets?

2 Explore Crashaw's use of *birds, nests, cold, warmth*.

3 Discuss the importance of stanzas 11 and 13 in the development of the ideas in the poem.

4 Read the poem aloud, following the indication that the chorus repeats the final couplet of stanzas 4–12. What does this add to your perception of the poem? Does it gain from being spoken by more than one or two voices?

5 Try to obtain and listen to a recording of Purcell's vocal music, such as *Come ye sons of art, rejoice*. Can you find a relationship between this kind of music and this poem?

Hymn to Saint Teresa

1 Discuss the purpose and effect of the opening one-and-a-half lines of the poem.

2 Examine the way in which Crashaw draws on images of childhood in lines 1–24 of the poem.

3 Bearing in mind the double meaning of the verb 'to die' (sexual climax) when used in some contexts by many sixteenth- and seventeenth-century poets, explore the use of the concept of death in the poem, especially between lines 81 and 120.

4 Evaluate the poem's success as a presentation of mystic experience and a reflection on the nature of passionate belief.

5 Find an illustration of Bernini's statue of Saint Teresa. There is one in Gombrich's **History of Western Art**. How does this visual image compare with images used by Crashaw?

Further Activities

1 Discuss the impression you gain from *Hymn of the Nativity* and *Hymn to Saint Teresa* of the nature of Crashaw's own religious beliefs and experience.

2 Examine the poetic forms used in both these poems. Why do you think they were chosen, and how well do they suit Crashaw's purposes?

3 How does Crashaw vary the rhythms within the body of a poem?

4 Explore the range of visual images offered in the two poems. Note those which you find most successful, those which you feel are less so, and consider your reasons for your evaluation.

5 What do you feel differentiates Crashaw from the other metaphysical poets whose work you have read, and where does that difference lie? How aware are you when reading of the poet's individual voice in these poems? What kind of voice is it?

Andrew Marvell

On a Drop of Dew

1 Analyse the rhyme scheme and metre of this poem, and note where you find that these change. Why do you think Marvell makes this shift? How does the alteration relate to the theme of the poem?

2 Note the pairing of ideas in the second half of the poem. What is their purpose?

3 How does Marvell express the idea of 'roundness' in the poem? Note the words he uses, and consider both their sound and their meaning.

Bermudas

1 Examine the ways in which Marvell uses images which relate to the senses. Note those which you find most effective, and consider why you have chosen them.

2 Do you think that Marvell is more interested in creating the hymn of praise to God or sensuous images of an earthly paradise? Or are the two inextricably linked?

3 Imagine the condition of the crew of a seventeenth-century sailing ship after months at sea. Is *Bermudas* an idealized picture? If so, why? (In *The Storm*, John Donne wrote about his experiences in such a vessel en route to the Azores:

Some coffined in their cabins lie, equally
Grieved that they are dead, and yet must die.)

The Nymph complaining for the death of her Fawn

1 Examine the means by which Marvell shapes the narrative of the poem.

2 In this poem, Marvell presents the subject speaking directly and telling her own story. How would you describe the speaker, and the way in which she speaks? Explore the ways in which she has been presented, analysing the diction of the poem and its structure, as well as the narrative.

3 What ideas do you think that Marvell is exploring through the story of this poem? How aware are you, as the reader, of the poet creating, selecting and presenting material for his purpose?

The Definition of Love

1 Make a note of the images which you have found to be similar to those used by other poets, and compare both the ways in which they are used, and how successful they are in furthering argument and communicating ideas.

2 How do you respond to this poem? Do you feel that the poet is simply playing with ideas and constructing a clever, witty argument, or can you detect a possible emotional base for it? If so, where does it lie?

To his Coy Mistress

1 Do you find the poem persuasive?

2 Read Donne's *To his Mistress Going to Bed* alongside this poem. As a wooing poem, which appeals to you most? Why? How does it compare with other such poems in this anthology?

3 How would you describe Marvell's tone here? Is he self-mocking, serious, or what?

4 Write a brief account of the theme and tone of each of the three verse paragraphs, noting how they relate to each other, and how they differ.

5 Note the effect of alliteration and assonance, especially in the final stages of the poem.

6 Note which images you find most forceful, interesting and original, and state your reasons.

7 Attempt to imitate Marvell's poetic style, and write a reply to this poem from the 'mistress'.

The Fair Singer

1 How do metre and rhyme contribute to the harmonies in this poem?

2 Trace the development of the imagery through the three stanzas.

The Picture of Little T.C. in a Prospect of Flowers

1 Analyse the structure and rhyme scheme of this poem. How do they help to provide a note of uncertainty in the presentation of the child?

2 Explore the imagery of the poem, and its relationship to the theme.

3 Where do you detect underlying questions about the child's future?

4 How does Marvell combine the ideas of the transience of spring and the fragility of human life?

The Garden

1 What is the poetic form used here? What is its effect? How does the rhythm of the poem reinforce its theme?

2 List the comparisons Marvell draws between the world of men and the world of the garden. Gather examples of both and judge how they compare, and for what purpose.

3 Compare the sensory images which you find in this poem with those you noted in *Bermudas*. How similar are they? Does Marvell use them in the same way in both poems?

4 How do you react to the images in stanza 5? How would you describe them?

5 Choose one stanza, and note where Maxwell uses monosyllables, disyllables and polysyllables. What kind of pattern can you find? Consider the effects achieved by the placing of words in this poem.

6 Working with a partner, share and discuss your ideas about what you

consider to be the theme of this poem. Then, individually, consolidate these into one short, succinct statement which expresses your own ideas.

An Horatian Ode

1 How do you react to the subject of this poem? Has Marvell aroused your admiration for Cromwell, or your sympathies for the king? Or both of these emotions? Discuss your reactions, and find support for them in the poem and the way in which it has been written.

2 Why do you think that Marvell has drawn on classical parallels? Note where they occur, how they are used, and how they relate to the purpose of the poem.

3 What is the effect of the very short lines?

4 As a Royalist or as a Parliamentarian, make a case for or against the inclusion of this poem in a definitive edition of Marvell's poetry.

Further Activities

1 Consider the aspects of Marvell's poetry which indicate the social, philosophical and political background against which it was written. Explore the ways in which the reader is made aware of this, and discuss how important you think it is to have some understanding of this in order to appreciate his writing fully.

2 Decide which of Marvell's poems appeal to you most, and the reasons why they do. Also, note where you find his writing less attractive. Find your own way of writing about your responses to him, and how to support what you say.

3 How do you evaluate Marvell's craftsmanship as a poet? Which features of his written style strike you as most individual and interesting?

4 Consider how Marvell uses the conceit as a means both to define and to argue. How does this compare with the use made of it by other poets whose work you have studied in this selection?

5 What similarities, and what differences, do you find in the work of Marvell and that of other poets in this anthology?

6 Marvell's writing has been described as combining wit and seriousness. Choose examples of his writing which you think might substantiate this claim.

Henry Vaughan

Regeneration

1 In this poem, Vaughan creates an allegorical account of a spiritual journey, using natural images of landscape and season. Explore these images, noting the ways in which he uses them to indicate the stages of his travel.

2 Make a careful examination of the fourth stanza to determine its importance in the overall structure of the argument.

3 Examine Vaughan's use of verbs, and the ways in which he chooses and uses them to explore experience.

The Retreat

1 Note the metre and rhyme scheme used in this poem. Why did Vaughan use this particular style, and what is its effect?

2 Consider the ways in which you become aware of the poet's emotions. How would you describe the emotions and desires which he expresses here?

3 Examine the conceits which you find in lines 6 and 20. How do they work and integrate with the overall meaning?

The Morning-watch

1 Explore the tensions created by the images of death and those of vigorous life. How do they contribute to your understanding of the poem?

2 A feature of Vaughan's writing is his unexpected use of words. What examples can you find in this poem? Find ways of expressing in your own writing what you have discovered about this feature of Vaughan's style.

3 Consider the effect of line length and metre in this poem.

4   Read Herbert's poem *Prayer (I)*, and compare it with this poem in terms of language, structure and ideas.

The Dawning

1   Analyse the line structure of the first verse paragraph, and note its effect. How does it compare with the second part of the poem?

2   Discuss the way in which the extended conceit based on images of water works in the second verse paragraph.

3   How would you describe the tone of this poem? In what ways is it similar to, and in what ways different from, *The Morning-watch*?

The World

1   Discuss the effect of the opening couplet. Why do you think that this is an oft-quoted image? What is its relationship to the rest of the poem?

2   List the different kinds of humanity which Vaughan selects as material for this poem. What does his choice tell you about his thinking?

3   Explore the language used to describe each kind of person. What is the individual distinction of each set of images? Note the sound, as well as the sense, in your investigation.

Man

1   Examine how Vaughan's use of varied line length and metre combines with the rhyme scheme, and its effect.

2   Discuss the ideas which this poem shares with *The World*, their similarities and differences.

3   Compare the way in which Vaughan uses the image of stones in the last stanza with a similar idea in the last stanza of Donne's *Nocturnal upon St Lucy's Day*.

4   Discuss the nature and effectiveness of the conceit with which Vaughan closes the poem. What do you think he means by it?

Cock-crowing

1   Explore the ways in which Vaughan uses the ideas of light and dark, sleeping and waking, watching and revelation, to develop his argument in this poem.

2 Discuss the methods which Vaughan uses to link mysticism and natural imagery.

3 Note the verse form, rhyme and metrical pattern. What effect do these have in establishing the tone of the poem?

The Night

1 Evaluate your response to this poem. Do you find it obscure and difficult to understand? If so, why? Do you find it possible to enjoy the poem without a complete knowledge of the ideas which underlie it?

2 Select the images which you find most effective, and assess the reasons for your choice.

3 How would you describe the poet's voice, and his feelings about his subject in this poem? What evidence backs your ideas?

The Waterfall

1 Read the poem aloud, and discuss the sound patterns which it creates, and their purpose. How does the form of the poem contribute to the exploration of its theme?

2 In this poem (as he does in many others) Vaughan uses contrasts as one method of exploring his ideas. How do they work here?

Further Activities

1 Make an assessment of the particular individuality of Vaughan as a poet, and explore ways of expressing this in your own writing.

2 Collect phrases and images from Vaughan's poems which strike you as apt, original or interesting. Note the context in which they were used, and the reason why you have chosen them.

3 Discuss the evidence for Herbert's influence on Vaughan which you can discover from the selections of both poets' writing in this collection.

4 If asked to explain what you understand by the assertion that Vaughan is a mystic poet, how would you respond?

5 From your reading of this selection, how would you describe Vaughan's main concerns and ideas?

6 Identify the aspects of Vaughan's writings which you find obscure, and those which communicate clearly to you. Consider and discuss what these poems have to offer to present-day readers, and the best way to approach them.

ESSAY TOPICS

This short selection provides some general essay titles which can be used as they stand, or adapted to provide a basis for more closely focused questions. It supplements the activities topics which appear earlier.

1 Does this poetry have a timeless appeal, or is it too firmly rooted in its own era to speak clearly to a present-day readership?

2 Examine the idea that the work of these poets is more to be admired for its powers of argument than for its lyrical attractions.

3 Discuss and illustrate the methods by which these poets analyse emotional experience.

4 'The purpose of the conceit is not to be admired, but to stimulate thought.' Do you agree?

5 Choose examples of the different kinds of poetic form to be found in this selection, and explore the uses which are made of them.

6 Choose one of the poets whose work appears here, and write an essay which attempts to define his individual voice, style and achievement.

7 What differences, and what similarities, have you found in the love poetry and the religious poetry of John Donne?

8 Compare the poetry of George Herbert with that of any other of the poets included here.

9 Explore the range of Marvell's poetry, attempting to discover whether there are recognizable constant features in poems on very different subjects.

10 Write about the way in which Vaughan draws on the natural world in his writing.

11 How do Carew's love lyrics compare with those of Donne and Marvell?

12 Discuss the individuality of Crashaw's religious poetry.

WRITING AN ESSAY
ABOUT POETRY

You own personal response to a poet and his or her work is of major importance when writing an essay on poetry, either as part of your course or as an examination question. However, this personal response needs to be based on a solid concept of how poetry works, so you must clearly show that you understand the methods the poet uses to convey the message and ideas of the poem to the reader. In most cases, unless it is relevant to your answer, you should not pad out your essay with biographical or background material.

Planning

Look carefully at the wording of the question. Underline the important words and ideas. Make sure you apply your mind to these key elements of the question and then explore them in the essay.

Bring all your knowledge of, and opinions on, a poet and his or her poetry to this first stage of writing. Brainstorm your ideas and always combine these thoughts in a plan that shows the development and intention of your answer. Your plan must outline the structure of your essay. In exam conditions, the plan and the direction of your comments may take you only a few minutes and should be little more than a way of laying out your ideas in order. However the plan must be an outline of how and where you are going to link your evidence to the opinions and concepts of the essay. Reject any ideas which are not relevant at the planning stage. Remember that your plan should be arranged around your ideas and not the chronological order of a poem or a poet's work, or your essay will be weakened.

Writing

Your introduction must implicitly or, if you wish, explicitly make the teacher or examiner realize that you understand the question.

Don't spend a lot of time spotting, defining and examining poetic techniques and form. If you do identify these features, then you must be sure of the poetic terms and be able to show why they are significant in the verse and to the poet's attempts to create a 'meaning' and a message.

Make absolutely sure that your answer is clear and that it tackles the issues in the question precisely. Try to offer points for discussion and apply your knowledge in an interesting way. Don't go ahead and disregard what the question asks you to write about, then write the essay you want to write. Don't waffle, don't write too elaborately or use terms vaguely; at the same time, don't be too heavy-handed with your views. Strive to put your opinions directly and accurately.

In exam conditions be aware of the time, and if you are running out of your allotted span then make sure that you put down your most important ideas in the minutes left. Try to leave a few minutes to revise and proof-read your script. Be sure that the points you have made make sense and are well supported by evidence. Don't try to introduce new ideas as you write unless they are essential to your essay. Often these extra thoughts can distract you from the logic of your argument. If it is essential, then refer back to your plan and slot the idea into the right part of the essay.

Quotations

Quotations are a vital source of evidence for the viewpoints and ideas you express in your essay. Try not to misquote and remember that when using extracts of more than a few words you should place them separately outside your text as they would be laid out in the poem.

If you follow the advice here you will produce a clear, relevant and logical essay. Try to spend time reading and listening to the comments of your teacher and make your own notes on your work for revision purposes.

Andrew Whittle

A NOTE FROM A CHIEF EXAMINER

Your examination script is the medium through which you communicate with your examiner. As a student, you will have studied what writers say and how they say it; your examiner will assess what *you* say and how you say it. This is the simple process through which your knowledge and understanding of the texts you have studied is converted into your examination result.

The questions which you will find on your examination paper have been designed to enable you to display your ability to engage in short, highly-concentrated explorations of particular aspects of the texts which you have studied. There is no intention to trick you into making mistakes, rather to enable you to demonstrate to your examiner your knowledge and understanding. Questions take a variety of forms. For a poetry text, you may be asked to concentrate on one poem, or a particular group of them, and provide detailed examination of some features of the writing. You may be asked to range widely throughout a poet's work, exploring specified aspects of his or her style and themes. You may be asked to provide a considered personal reaction to a critical evaluation of the poet's work.

Whatever the question, you are, ultimately, being asked to explore *what* and *how*, *content* and *style*. Equally, you are being asked for a personal response. You are communicating to your examiner your own understanding of the text, and your reactions to it, based on the studies you have undertaken.

All of this may seem very simple, if not self-evident, but it is worthwhile to devote some time to thinking about what an examination is, and how it works. By doing so, you will understand why it is so important that you should prepare yourself for your examination in two principal ways: first, by thorough, thoughtful and analytical textual study, making your own well-informed evaluation of the work of a particular writer, considering what he or she is conveying to you, how this is done, how you react, and what has made you respond in that way; then, by practising the writing skills which you will need to convey all these things to your examiner.

When assessing your script and awarding marks, examiners are working to guidelines which instruct them to look for a variety of different qualities in an essay.

These are some of the things which an examiner will consider.

- How well has the candidate understood the essay question and the given task? Is the argument, and the material used to support it, entirely relevant?

- Is quotation used aptly, and textual reference employed skilfully in discussion?

- Is the candidate aware of how and why the writer has crafted material in a particular way?

- Is there evidence of engagement with the text, close analytical reading, and awareness of subtleties in interpretation?

- Does the candidate have the necessary vocabulary, both general and critical, to express his or her understanding lucidly? Are technical terms integrated into discussion?

- Can the candidate provide an interesting, clearly-expressed and structured line of argument, which fully displays a well-informed personal response?

From these points, you should be able to see the kind of approach to examination questions which you should avoid. Re-hashed notes, second-hand opinion, unsupported assertion and arid copies of marginal jottings have no place in a good script. Don't fall into the trap of reproducing a pre-planned essay. Undoubtedly you will find (if your preparation has been thorough) that you are drawing on ideas which you have already explored in other essays, but all material used must be properly adapted to the task you are given. Don't take a narrative approach; paraphrase cannot replace analysis. Do not, under any circumstances, copy out chunks of introduction or critical notes from your text in an open book examination. Nor do you need to quote at excessive length; your examiner knows the text.

It is inevitable that, when writing in examination conditions, you will only use quite a small amount of the material you have studied in order to answer a particular question. Don't feel that what you are not using has been wasted. It hasn't. All your studies will have informed the understanding you display in a succinct, well-focused answer, and will equip you to write a good essay.

Virginia Graham

Chief Examiner for A-level English

SELECT BIBLIOGRAPHY

Critical editions of the major works of Donne, Marvell, Herbert and Vaughan (these in one volume) are published in paperback by Oxford University Press.

Biographies

John Donne, Life, Mind and Art John Carey, Faber (1981)

Henry Vaughan Stevie Davies, Seren Press (1995)

Both these biographies link the poets' lives with their writing, and are entertaining and lively to read.

The most full and accessible biographies of Herbert and Marvell are probably the following:

A Life of George Herbert Amy M. Charles, Cornell University Press (1977)

(Marvell) *The Poet's Time* W. Chernaik, Cambridge (1983)

There is a great deal of critical literature on metaphysical poetry, and the following suggestions offer only a few titles which are generally accessible, from libraries or publishers.

English Poetry of the Seventeenth Century George Parfait, Longman (1992)

A generic approach, focusing on types of poetry (e.g. lyric, satire) in the context of its age: includes an interesting chapter on poetry by women.

The School of Donne A. Alvarez (1961)

Though there has been new thinking since the time this book was first published, it offers some interesting insights.

Five Metaphysical Poets Joan Bennett, Cambridge University Press (1963)

Selected Essays T. S. Eliot, Faber

The Metaphysical Poets (ed.) Helen Gardner, Penguin

A wide selection of poetry, and an important introductory essay.

Kissing the Rod Greer, Medoff, Sansome and Hastings (1988)

An anthology of seventeenth-century verse written by women.

INDEX OF FIRST LINES

A ward, and still in bonds, one day	171
Ah! what time wilt thou come? when shall that cry	179
All after pleasures as I rid one day	59
All kings, and all their favourites	23
As virtuous men pass mildly away	33
Ask me no more where Jove bestows	109
At the round earth's imagined corners, blow	43
Batter my heart, three-personed God; for, you	45
Blasted with sighs, and surrounded with tears	25
Busy old fool, unruly sun	15
By our first strange and fatal interview	3
Can we not force from widowed poetry	99
Come, Madam, come, all rest my powers defy	1
Come, we shepherds whose blest sight	113
Death be not proud, though some have called thee	43
Death, thou wast once an uncouth hideous thing	83
Father of lights! what sunny seed	187
For God's sake hold your tongue, and let me love	17
Give me more love, or more disdain	105
Go, and catch a falling star	11
Had we but world enough, and time	149
Happy those early days! when I	175
Having been tenant long to a rich Lord	85
Holiness on the head	67
How soon doth man decay!	79
How vainly men themselves amaze	155
I am a little world made cunningly	47
I have done one braver thing	13
I know the ways of Learning; both the head	71
I made a posy, while the day ran by	77
I saw Eternity the other night	183
I struck the board, and cried, No more	91
I wonder, by my troth, what thou, and I	9
If the quick spirits in your eye	107
Let man's soul be a sphere, and then, in this	49
Let me pour forth	27

Lord, how can man preach thy eternal word? 57
Lord, thou art absolute sole Lord 121
Love bade me welcome: yet my soul drew back 95
Mark but this flea, and mark in this 7
Mark how the bashful morn, in vain 107
Mark you the floor? that square and speckled stone 57
My God, I heard this day 73
My Love is of a birth as rare 147
O joys! Infinite sweetness! with what flowers 177
O my chief good 61
Oh, to vex me, contraries meet in one 49
Prayer the Church's banquet, angels' age 69
Rise heart; thy Lord is risen. Sing his praise 63
See how the orient dew 135
See with what simplicity 153
Since she whom I loved hath paid her last debt 47
So, so, break off this last lamenting kiss 41
Sweetest love, I do not go 19
Take heed of loving me 39
The forward youth that would appear 161
The wanton troopers riding by 139
This is my play's last scene, here heavens appoint 41
Through that pure Virgin-shrine 191
'Tis the year's midnight, and it is the day's 29
To make a final conquest of all me 151
Twice or thrice had I loved thee 21
Weighing the steadfastness and state 185
What if this present were the world's last night? 45
When first my lines of heav'nly joys made mention 67
When first thou didst entice to thee my heart 85
When God at first made man 81
When my devotions could not pierce 89
When my grave is broke up again 37
When thou, poor excommunicate 105
Where the remote Bermudas ride 137
Who says that fictions only and false hair 65
Whoever comes to shroud me, do not harm 35
Wilt thou forgive that sin where I begun 53
With what deep murmurs through time's silent stealth 195

Printed in the USA
CPSIA information can be obtained
at www.ICGtesting.com
JSHW01193525102 3
50883JS00016B/41